T0149500

Women Seeking Shelter

The Life and Times of Three Sarahs
1806-1955

JEAN ROMANO

iUniverse LLC
Bloomington

Women Seeking Shelter
THE LIFE AND TIMES OF THREE SARAHS 1806-1955

iUniverse books may be ordered through booksellers or by contacting:

iUniverse
1663 Liberty Drive
Bloomington, IN 47403
www.iuniverse.com
1-800-Authors (1-800-288-4677)

ISBN: 978-1-4917-0263-5 (sc)
ISBN: 978-1-4917-0264-2 (e)

Printed in the United States of America.

iUniverse rev. date: 8/5/2013

Table of Contents

ILLUSTRATIONS

Maternal Line: A Family Tree

PICTURES

With Many Thanks to

Joan Alexis Hughes Altgelt who led the family into Ancestry and all the surprises it held! Joan is a master detective and map creator, inspiration and supporter. Many thanks also to Marilyn Kraft Wooton, another cousin who was the keeper of memorabilia and Louise Hughes Plank, the memory maven. A special thanks to Joyce Emery Kinney, recorder of all things Eastport.

The Old Sow

The cover picture was taken by Jim Lowe of Eastport, Maine, master of photography and aerial maps of the area. The Old Sow is considered the largest whirlpool in the western hemisphere. It is found in the Bay of Fundy near Deer Island but I have seen it from the coast of Eastport. It is tidal and powerful with a trench as deep as 400 feet. For me it symbolizes the swirling events of history, it is awesome, unpredictable, and a part of one family's heritage.

Preface

This history spans three centuries. At the beginning of the 19th century, health care, old age assistance, unions, and a regulated work place were absent. Education and transportation were not an implicit part of governments. Newspapers were important and the source of local and national events. The slow move towards social programs during the early 1900's was linked to economic growth, war, and globalization. The 21st century shows signs of a return to individualistic thinking and a push to return to less governmental regulation and support. This new century wavers between the power of the market versus the power of government and the working class. In times of economic stress, the expansion of government may be supported, as happened in the 1930's when the last generation of the three women in this story were born.

The lives of all the women were altered by conflicts and wars. The Revolutionary War, the War of 1812, war with Mexico, the Civil War and the two World Wars gave women the chance to show their ability to handle many of the men's responsibilities as well as their own. Differences and similarities are present in the lives of each generation. Some reactions to life are handed down through experiences of the women before them and all are affected by the social history around them. Some of the women lived in more than one century and their changing values sprang from their own struggles to survive. Their children's success was not always welcomed as the family became smaller and geographically separated. Women especially felt the impact of change.

The role of homemaker was redefined during World War I and gaining the right to vote affected the country's move towards women's issues from that time forward. During the period from 1847 until the present, 134 armed conflicts involving the United States were recorded and this number does not include the many battles with Indian tribes. Conflict was part of the daily consciousness as it is today. Some wars affected only a small part of the country, others wrapped the whole nation into the actions of the military. Through the years, the men of the family went to war. By the 1940's, at least one female family member was part of a war effort officially, although other women actively participated in earlier conflicts.

As usually happens, the pattern in the early years is of the men as the hunter-gatherers and the women as providers of shelter for the family unit. It is not unusual for women to push for a better life, sometimes material and often of the spirit. This family story begins with Sarah Morang, born in Lubec, Maine in 1806. Her father was born in St. Pierre du Sud, Canada and he married Martha Denbow of Lubec. An investigation on Martha is still underway, but for the time, we will consider Martha the woman who married a Canadian and built a life in Maine. Together these two young people made the change from Canada to New England in a time when loyalties to Crown or country were shifting and dividing families.

This was an age before canned formula, washers, driers or disposable diapers. None of the three Sarahs had these amenities. Sarah Morang's daughter, Sarah Ann, sent a young husband off to war, bore eleven children, moved a family from Maine to Long Island and died far from her birth place. Not all of her children lived but she named her youngest daughter Sarah and the story continues. The third Sarah, daughter of Sarah Ann, moved farthest from the family roots in Maine but the same traditions, world and national issues continued to affect her life.

One family member, Joan Alexis Altgelt, has approached this family story through a study of factual ancestry, I have looked at it as part of the history of the times, imagining what was done through comments, memories, books and articles. Where and when they lived affected everyone who followed. Why some events took place is usually by no choice of their own and there is no way of knowing how much influence the Sarahs had on the course of their journeys. It is a story of women, and since most recorded history documents men, part of the story is an educated guess.

For women, wars often gave impetus to greater liberty and voice in societies. This small picture in time begins after the Revolutionary War and the start of the United

States of America. The 19th century is heavily influenced by the actions of women during the war years and the need for women to be educated in order to raise a new generation of knowledgeable citizens. Each new war, and there were many, large and small, brought sacrifice and gains for women. Despite the tremendous efforts of women in the workplace during WWII, it was not until the 1950's that their status came into the discussion. There were jobs, but few with career ladders for women, an issue addressed by the Civil Rights Act of 1954, Title VII, passed under Lyndon B. Johnson's administration.

At that time, the Equal Opportunities Commission felt race was the major civil rights concern. It was the action of women stewardesses who brought a suit to the EOC that registered age and gender discrimination as civil rights denied, most especially to women. Another suit was filed by Lorena Weeks against Southern Bell telephone and resulted in a ruling of no male only jobs. Still, gays and black women were left behind in the '50's.

No one lives in a vacuum. Although their awareness of the rest of the world had not reached the proportions the global network affords as now, the women of the past were part of world-wide changes. The most important question is always the idea of progress—each generation becoming better educated, housed, fed and clothed. Each new generation living in times of peace and justice that exceed that of their ancestors. Progress is in the eye of the beholder but the legacies of past times are glaringly evident in the start of the 21st century.

MATERNAL LINE OF THREE SARAHS

Alexander Morang (1768-1860)
son of Jean François Morang & Rosalie Forêt

b. St. Pierre de la Rivière du Sud, Quebec, Canada
[bet. Montmagny & Quebec City]
d. Lubec, Maine
m. 1790 in Eastport, Maine, **Martha Denbow** (1760-1850)
b. Canada d. Lubec, Maine

Sarah E. Morang (1806-1892)
daughter of Alexander Morang & Martha Denbow
b. Canada d. Eastport, Maine
m. 1827 in Lubec, **Nathaniel MacDonald** (1801-aft 1870)
b. Lubec d. Eastport, Maine
Children: John Allen (1826-1896); Olive (1828);
Nathaniel Jr. (1830-1906);
Damietta (1832-1909); Francis (1834-1836);
William (1835-1860);
Moses (1837); George (1838-1911); **Sarah Ann**
(1841-1915); Marietta (1843);
Hannah M. (1846-1847); Grace (1848-1920)

Sarah Ann MacDonald (1841-1915)
daughter of Sarah E. Morang & Nathaniel MacDonald
b. West Lubec, Maine d. New Village, Suffolk, New York
m. 1861 in Eastport, Maine, **Frederick Augustus Emery**
(1838-1915)
Children: Eugenia (1862); Hilton Frederick (1863);
Beatrice Mary (1865-1960);

Edwin Stanton (1867-1905); Portia Augusta (1869-1932);
Damietta [Henrietta] (1875-1963); George W. (1878-1950);
Sarah Matilda (1880-1955); Everett Milton (1884-1946)

Sarah Matilda Emery (1880-1955)
daughter of Sarah Ann MacDonald & Frederick Augustus Emery
b. Eastport, Maine d. Hackettstown, NJ
m. 1904 in Brooklyn, NY, **Reginald Corbitt Hughes**
(1873-1953)
b. Annapolis Royal, Nova Scotia d. Hackettstown, NJ
Children: Marjorie (1907-2001); Kenneth Emery
(1910-1965); Hilton Frederick (1912-2000);
Doris (1914-1998); George Alexander (1916-1997);
Louise (1922-)

This chart was devised by Joan Altgelt, using the Ancestry site.

I

The Nineteenth Century: The Global Picture

In 1806, the year Sarah Morang was born, the middle class in several European countries was struggling to gain political power. In France, England, and the American colonies, revolutions took place and ended for a time in 1815 with Napoleon's exile to Elba. The revolution in France looked towards universal suffrage, constitutional government and social and economic liberty. It also was the spark leading to nationalism. Germany was still in the process of nationalization, the major players were Britain, France and Spain with the Netherlands and Austria as players in the power struggles. The influence of these times on the newly formed United States drove the push towards independence in 1776.

Equally important was the rise of industrialization made possible by the use of new power resources: steam and later, electricity. Two classes were formed by the factory system: factory owners and workers. The belief in economic liberalism fostered the idea that unrestricted competition would result in the rise of powerful industries and the whole of the society would benefit. This is a question still unanswered but in the 19th century, in Europe and in the United States, men united and fought for their rights to a decent wage and hours. The women worked well into the 20th century for minimal wages, piece work rates, and in unsafe conditions but they also took part in union activities although rarely in leadership roles.

Early on, political movements were attached to the rise of industry. Democracy was the dominant movement in Europe, most especially in France and Great Britain. Only in Spain, Italy, Ireland, and Portugal were movements towards democracy and even Home Rule proceeding at a snail's pace. Germany had a system that concentrated power in an autocratic, efficient and military state with little voice for its citizens. In Russia, there was no attempt to hide the powers of despotism. Democracy was ascendant in the new United States and Great Britain.

Ireland and Scotland were part of the British Empire and a constant concern to many for human rights abuses. Ireland bred writers, politicians and national leaders who fought for religious freedom, land and property rights, political voice and human dignity. In the late 19th century the "evictions" brought much misery to the Irish people, leaving them homeless and hungry. The legal age for child labor was eight years of age. And famine was only one scourge, everything led to an impossible situation for most of the Irish and the result was the mass immigration of many to America and the docks of New York. This included the MacDonalds of this family tree who chose to locate in Maine.

Undercurrents of racism and anti-Semitism grew and were accepted even by the most creative and educated. The Dreyfus case fostered hatred against Jewish citizens and provided a premonition of times ahead.

The abolition of slavery came in 1834 in Britain. The newly formed United States almost disintegrated through Civil War over the same issue in 1861.

Latin America was very much a part of Down East history. The economy was stagnant from 1820-1850 and the mining sector was impacted by the wars of independence. Transportation and port facilities were undeveloped and investment capital was lacking. The defeat of Napoleon, the dependency on foreign markets kept the old order firmly in place and as happened in Quebec, land was the basis of wealth and prestige

After 1850, the population of Latin America doubled and demand for Latin American products resulted in capitalist expansion, largely in Europe.

One definitive event forever links the third Sarah to the sub-continent for her future husband's father, a mariner, died at sea on a routine trading passage. Plague was a constant for the sailors long at sea. While many found their grave in the waters of the Atlantic, George Alexander Hughes was buried in Rio de Janeiro. The trips between the Caribbean Islands and South America were frequent and the deaths at sea by those who made those voyages were expected.

Throughout the 19th century Latin America maintained independence but in many ways, the area functioned in economic dependency on the West, which provided the capital for economic expansion and owned many of the industries.

President Monroe challenged Spain in 1823, determined to stop the commercial monopolies held by other nations. Monroe, Jefferson, Madison and John Quincy Adams, agreed on the foreign policy principle of backing the freedom of the Latin American Republics. The British government joined in this effort known in the future as the Monroe Doctrine.

The industrialized European countries spent much time tempting China to enter the new world economy in the late 18th century and early 19th century. The Chinese saw little to gain in trade but were concerned with the growing military power of the West. Losses in a series of confrontations resulted in a forced acceptance of treaties that opened Chinese ports to European and then American and Japanese traders. In addition, land in port or treaty cities had to be turned over to foreigners residing in China. Chinese were excluded from areas controlled by foreigners. British, French, German, American and Japanese resided and claimed significant amounts of land in China by the early 19th century. The Chinese government was also forced to allow Western Christian missionaries into the interior of the country.

District magistrates were responsible for the welfare, control, and taxation of an average of 250,000 people. The magistrate's allegiance was to their localities and families, not the state, leading to internal rebellions after a series of natural catastrophes and man-made disasters made worse by over-reclamation of wet-lands, lowlands and mountain slopes.

Chinese people found a way to emigrate and entered as the major labor force during the thrust to build railroads in the western United States.

In the first half on the 19th century, Japan was basically an agricultural economy.

An unproductive samurai class was a most privileged part of the society. This led to a weak country, suffering increasing intrusions by Western powers. The policy of isolation that resulted limited technological advances and restricted global trade.

In 1825, foreign ships were barred from Japanese waters and in 1837 the American merchant ship Morrison was fired on and forced to leave. Anti-western policies followed and were applied to American, European and Russian ships that attempted entry.

The efforts of Commodore Perry to open trade began in 1853. He came to the port near the capital in Edo Bay with four ships and an ultimatum. On his return in 1854 the Kanawaga Treaty was signed, opening two ports for coal and supplies. It opened a pathway for trade.

The Meiji Restoration began a period of modernization. In 1868, Japan opened its borders and invited foreign advisors to assist in growth of technology and other areas of Western knowledge. The lessons were assimilated but the imports brought a distinctly Japanese society into being. However, the end of the samurai warrior class began the emergence of Japan into the modern era with a national military might capable of challenging the United States in 1941.

In the first half of the 19th century, the East India Company ruled on behalf of Britain. One member of the Company's Council, Thomas Macaulay, wrote in 1835 that the goal of British presence in India was 'to raise a class of persons, Indian in blood and colour, but English in taste, in opinions in morals and in intellect". Education, however, was for only a few as the bulk of Company profits were spent on its armed forces. The economy in India became stagnant although European influence in Calcutta, Madras and Bombay created a new Indian intelligentsia. Their intellectual life centered on the authority of the Brahmins, doctrines of caste separation and tradition, not on the values intended by the British.

Meanwhile, the lot of the peasants was harsh and compounded by heavy taxes. For the upper class, the occupation was disruptive and often resulted in deposed aristocrats and noble families. There was less and less support for the Company.

The Rebellion of 1857 was headed by a large portion of the Indian army and directed firmly at the British authorities. Soldiers shot their British officers and marched on Delhi. The mutiny spread and many died on both sides of the fighting. After the rebellion, a new Royal Government replaced the Company and by and the second half of the century technology produced a great railway system, major canals, steamships and the opening of the Suez canal. Indian owned textile mills helped break the stagnation of the early 1800's.

Universities, colleges and schools were opened through Indian administration and English. Native languages were used to develop the economy and the national culture that led to modern India. Today many services are outsourced to India and the expertise of a rising generation of technologists is unquestioned.

During the 19th century the diverse cultures of sub-Saharan Africa prevented a unified voice from arising to combat the influx of Europeans. The artificial borders drawn by the various European countries had no relationship to the ethnicity of the peoples within the boundaries set by the colonial governments. In 1804, Great Britain ended the slave trade and it ended slavery in its colonies in 1834. Britain patrolled the coast to stop slave ships, but between 1807 and 1888, close to 3 million

Africans were shipped overseas, usually to work for large farms in Cuba and Brazil.

The United States was a part of the slave trade—a commodity that built the wealth of the south. The country paid dearly for it with the Civil War.

The Muslim religion of West Africa was established in 1804 through the Sokoto Caliphate based on the lower Niger. Trade within the continent and as far away as Egypt and Brazil flourished. Through the Brazil connection, Down East ships were also connected to the African continent's trade.

The Middle East-European Imperialism

The slow weakening of the Ottoman Empire led Europeans to refer to it as the "sick man" and plans to conquer the area were quick to follow.

Russia, always looking for a warm water port, had long seen the straits that connected the Black Sea and the Mediterranean Sea—the Bosporus and the Dardanelles as an answer. In 1853 a small dispute between Russian and the Ottoman Empire started the Crimean War. Both Britain and France sent troops to support the Empire but although the Empire won, it was even weaker than before the conflict.

Both Britain and France held shares in the Suez Canal Company, the waterway between England and India. In the 1870's Britain took control of the Company and troops were dispatched to Egypt to guard the canal. Until 1922, Egypt remained under British control.

Foreign loans tied to the military ambitions of France and Britain weakened the Qajar Empire in Persia during this time. The great rivalries for power had a lasting impact on both Africa and the Middle East.

Issues to Come

The 19th century began with a search for power by many countries. Although the abolition of the slave trade was a positive note, the imperialism of the European nations is noted for the absolute certainty exhibited in their right to colonize, profit from and govern lands abroad. By 1884, a meeting was arranged in Berlin to set the rules for claiming colonies and the end of the century demonstrated the effects of the past actions. In 1879, Britain seized the Khyber Pass to complete its domination of Afghanistan. The Anglo-Boer War spanned both centuries (1899-1902), and the division of Persia into spheres of influence by Britain and Russia began the 20th century in the Middle East.

In China and Japan, isolation was ending by choice or by the entrance of Western powers into the orient. The influence of France, England and Germany became part of the culture of many countries who rebelled in diverse ways. India was most successful in creating the culture mix that would make it a technological powerhouse in the 21st century.

At the start of a new century in 2000, no one could predict the exact events facing the United States and the world. All of the indications present in the previous century gave clues to what would happen next. The oppression of some peoples and many countries led to uprisings across the globe and no one place is exempted from violence. The inclusion of women as decision makers is surely a hopeful sign: they remember well how long a wait it was for recognition.

As predicted by historians and other scholars, the rise of one civilization over another is part of a cycle. Wars and a wealth of resources gave the United States an edge over Europe as the 19th century grew old. The rise and decline of the powerful is well documented since recorded time began.

It is hard to tell how much of the world's events were known by the first Sarah. However, although news came late, the Eastport Sentinel began printing in 1818 during the British Occupation. Publication was sporadic until Maine became a State. A regular column in all local papers was arrivals and departures of shipping in the Maritimes, from Saint John to Eastport and Lubec. Their ships sailed to Trinidad, Cuba, Argentina, along the eastern coast and during the Gold Rush, around the Cape or to the Isthmus. Seemingly isolated, the Down East residents were more aware of the rest of the world than their in-land fellow citizens.

When gold was discovered in California, ships from Eastport and other Maine ports set sail around the Cape for the mother lode in the west. Some also took their passengers to Panama to allow foot passage across to the Pacific. Stories came home to Eastport and the world seemed smaller every year.

As has been noted by Joyce Kinney, Eastport has Canadian Islands on three sides: Campobello on the east, Indian Island to the north and Deer Island on the northwest. It was also easy travel across the border to St. John's and the rivers that traveled inland. Eastport itself is an island, an early name for the town is Moose Island. Canadian and American fishermen brought herring to the sardine factories of Eastport and salesmen and city dwellers found Eastport a refreshing change from the heat of their homes. All brought an international flavor to the small town.

In the early 20th century, smuggling in of both Chinese men and opium was part of the Eastport scene. The Chinese who left their own country were wealthy men who had relatives in the United States. They usually disembarked in St. John where they waited for the next leg of their journey into Eastport or Machias and then into the interior.

Eastport, Maine was not a backwater. It was not isolated from the greater world and its families were far more sophisticated than the early settlers who headed for the mid-west.

II

St. Pierre Du Sud and Port Royal: The Beginning of Sarah Morang's Story

The influence of French Quebec seems unlikely in this American story but Quebec du Sud is closer to Maine than to the rest of Canada or the United States. Alexander Morang, the son of Jean Francois Morang, was born in Quebec in 1765. By 1774 the Quebec Act of had extended the province as far west as the Mississippi, and although French customary law was allowed, the British crown held the land, giving access to trade and military routes across the Great Lakes.

While the Morang family were well settled in St. Pierre-de-la-Riviere-du-Sud, Montmagny, northeast of Quebec City, Jean Francois married a young woman born in Port Royal, Nova Scotia, Rosalie De Forest (Forêt). Port Royal is a town about 8 kilometers from Annapolis Royal and it is still a farming community and home to a replica of the first settlement when it was the capital of the colony of Acadia. The history of the expulsion of the Acadians is memorialized in Evangeline, a poem by Henry Wadsworth Longfellow. The story itself is not poetry but tragic prose.

The parents of Rosalie and her grandparents as well were early settlers, probably relocated from farming communities in western France. As far back as records can be traced in the early 17th century, these folks had their homes in Port Royal. By 1654 the English stopped French immigration. The Acadian-Cajun Genealogy and History Website details many stages of Acadia as it moved between English and French rule. From 1709 until 1748, Acadians became true Nova Scotians and many remained neutral during the wars. Nevertheless, beginning in 1749 they were driven out of Nova Scotia, New Brunswick, Prince Edward Island and parts of Maine. They were shipped by boat far from their homes, and often separated from their families in the process. To ensure no returns, the English burned homes, crops and livestock leaving barren land where the Acadians had lived.

Rosalie Forest was born in Port Royal in 1745 at the end of the period of peace and prosperity. Although many Acadians were relocated to Louisiana and are documented under Cajun Genealogy lines, the de Forests moved across the Bay to Quebec. It is not known exactly when they took this journey but they remained intact as a family and brought their culture with them to the Canadian mainland. And so war is the impetus for the movement of the first women of one family of French heritage, seeking shelter in the new world.

After the Revolutionary War in the Thirteen Colonies, Loyalist refugees changed the demographics of Quebec by bringing a significant number of English speaking Protestants to a place formerly French speaking and Catholic. While Canada grappled with questions of religion and language, the vestiges of the American Revolution continued to play a part in the country's development. King and Crown or loyalty to France were the issues that led to the unique nature of Canada today. The clash of language and culture has settled down in the 21st century and Canada successfully educates bilingual children. It is a sovereign country now but in the late 18th century, the future of the land mass was undecided.

There are probably many reasons why Alexander Morang's father and mother left Quebec for Lubec, Maine, sometime after his birth in 1765. Rosalie and Alexander raised thirteen children over the years with home a place that often changed. The proximity of the Maritimes encouraged interaction and movement as the three areas were closely connected by trade and occupation. The Morong's seventh child, Pierre, was born in Miramichi, New Brunswick Canada in 1775 so the family was already on the move. The vast reaches of the St. Lawrence River did much to connect Quebec with both the Maritimes and with Maine. The political influences surely included allegiances to Britain or France but economic factors were most likely reasons for movement. For Rosalie, her duties were to her children, her allegiances followed her husband's journeys.

The early 19th century saw the timber industry replace the fur trade as the mainstay of the economy in British North America. Napoleon Bonaparte's blockade of Europe switched Britain's wood source from Scandinavia to Canada. The wood was needed for ships to continue the fight against Napoleon. Both St. John, New Brunswick and Quebec City loaded oak and elm onto hundreds of ships bound for Great Britain. In "lower" Canada, land became more and more difficult to wrest from the entrenched seigneurial regime. These seigneurs demanded higher and higher rents, creating a shortage of land for farming.

Many were forced to move into towns to find work, or across borders to Maine where work could be found in harvesting and preparing lumber or in ship building and related industries. Fishing as a career was a natural part of the Maritimes. The closeness of water from rivers, bays, inlets and the ocean itself shaped the lifestyle of those who chose that part of the country and the lifestyle in Maine and Canada was similar.

A map can show a triangle from Nova Scotia, Lubec and Montmagny, the homes of Rosalie Forest Morang. The St. Lawrence acted as highway in those times when road maps were still to come and fast travel meant by water, not land.

While the Morangs and their children looked south for a home that would provide work, shelter and peace, other families that would become part of theirs were following the same path.

Nathaniel Denbow and Liddy Tibbetts Denbow, were married in Eastport, Maine. The original spelling was Denbo, changed in the 18th century to Denbow. Their marriage in 1767 was fruitful. Seven children were raised by Nathaniel and Liddy. Their daughter Martha, who was mother to the first of our Sarahs, was born in Canada around 1760. It is another family moving easily between two widely diverse countries, perhaps passing in transit and finally united by marriage.

The marriage of Martha Denbow and Alexander Morang on October 10, 1790 was a final step towards establishing the Morang family in Maine. Alexander was a cooper by trade. The health of his family is a tribute to his ability to feed, house and clothe them through difficult times. The mystery of four years between the second and third child, however, asks for possible answers.

Their marriage was long and marked by a growing and extended family. On a count, fourteen children are found in Maine records and Ancestry Family Trees vaguely mention the arrival of new babies from 1791–1818. Martha herself would have been 58 when the last child was born, a standing record for the family then and now! When they married, Martha was 30 years of age, Alexander was 21. Rosalie, their first daughter, was born a year after the wedding and named for Alexander's mother. A second baby, Francis, was born in 1792 but four years elapsed before the birth of Margaret. The twins born in 1798 died in infancy but in 1799 Samuel joined the family and in 1802, John, 1804, Anna and then in 1806, Sarah. From 1809 until 1818 five new siblings were included in the family. Martha spent 27 years raising and bearing her children.

Martha died of Palsy in Lubec in 1850 in her 90th year. Alexander outlived her by ten years and died the year before the start of the Civil War.

Sarah Morang was born in Lubec, the ninth born child of this large family. It is not known if her grandparents, Jean Francois and Rosalie Morang had joined her father and his family in Lubec at the time of her birth. Her mother's family were still residents of Lubec early in the 18th century. It is certainly hoped that Martha had help.

Martha's sister, Elizabeth, born in 1777, married Gilbert Morang in 1800, providing another close family link, as he was the brother of Alexander. Although records show Gilbert's birth in St. Pierre Du Sud in 1777, Elizabeth is firmly rooted in Lubec where they made their home.

Tracing the time of the Morang family exodus from Quebec is difficult. It seems that the Morang (Morin) family left as a unit somewhere between 1765 and 1800 as both Jean Francoise and Rosalie died in Lubec in 1820. Their son Alexander and Martha Denbow were married in Eastport on October 10th, 1790. Martha was 30 at the time of her wedding; her mother-in-law had married at age 15.

Lubec was certainly the home of the families Denbow and Morang in this period. It was a hub in the region and before Eastport broke away to become a town of its own, Lubec was of considerable size. There was work for those involved in any part of the life of the sea.

III

Lubec

Lubec is close to Eastport now and at one time the two were one town. Its close proximity to the Canadian Maritimes set its course for trade, fishing and herring processing and the shipping industry. Lubec is in the most south-easterly part of Washington County and Quoddy Head is the most south-easterly point of both the state of Maine and the United States.

The story carries on as the development of Lubec came in a period of peace in Nova Scotia for the Acadians did not assure peace for all. In 1716, a permanent settlement was undertaken by Colonel John Allan and others who were patriot fugitives from Cumberland County, Nova Scotia. "Flaggs Point" existed where Lubec Village now stands. Louis F. Delesdernier and Nehemiah Small, who fled Eastport when it was occupied by the British, appear to be the first permanent settlers. Some of the earliest inhabitants were people of French origin who came from

Nova Scotia in1758. The French left for Lower Canada and the upper parts of the St. John River soon after.

A Congregational Church was established in1820, through the diligent work of Reverend Elijah Kellogg. Reverend Andrew Bigelow was ordained the first pastor in 1821. By the 1820's the churches in town consisted of two of the Christians and one Methodist, Baptist and The Disciples. There were 10 public schoolhouses. By the year 1880, 2,109 residents made up the official census count.

From the early 18th century until the present day, ties of family, friends and commerce with New Brunswick are evident. Passamaquoddy Bay linked Lubec to Eastport. The name of the Bay, translated from the tribal language of the Passamaquoddy tribe, means "pollack plenty place" and the 95 miles of shoreline encouraged people to build homes and form a community.

North Lubec and Moose Island were incorporated as the town of Eastport in 1798 with 588 inhabitants. On June 21, 1811, Lubeck (sp) was successfully separated from Eastport by petition. This has caused some considerable thought when researching earlier records.

Much illicit trade happened in this border region and President Washington organized the Revenue Cutter Service in 1790 to curb its success. The Cutter Service later became the United States Coast Guard. Despite this effort, the fishermen of Lubec and Eastport knew the area waters and tides, isolated coves and islands too well to be curtailed. The location of Campobello and Deer Islands made the work of customs officers and the Cutter Service almost impossible.

As Campobello is a stone's throw from Lubec, it would not be a difficult move. The history of the times shows no particular economic reason for leaving Maine. There may be more political reasons for the move. Maine lies to the west of Charlotte County. History and geography link the county's families to Nova Scotia and coastal Maine. Charlotte was settled in 1785 by Loyalists and Quakers. The boundary between New Brunswick and Maine had been in dispute since the American Revolution and this dispute was not over until the British claim was verified. At this point, Calais, Maine and St. Stephen, New Brunswick appear to have no set boundaries. A resident describes it in the Charlotte County website as "one big town with a bridge in the middle".

The contraband trade flourished in Campbello where wharves full of British manufactured goods were exchanged for cash, beef, port, flour and wood products. By 1820, the year Maine separated from Massachusetts to become the 23rd state; the road from Lubec to Machias was complete and open for stage coach travel.

The rise of ship-building in the area was a boon to a place with a natural port, enormous amounts of timber and plentiful labor. Blacksmiths, carpenters, coopers, ship-chandlers and other related workmen came to the area to help launch the 20 vessels completed between 1804 and 1830. Tide power, at times rising 15 feet tall, sparked plaster mills and other manufacturing.

The biggest boost to Lubec was the growth of the sardine industry as the Franco-Prussian War stopped the importation of those small herring. For two decades, beginning in 1880, 23 sardine factories were built in

Lubec, lining the waterfront with employers and a special fragrance. It offered employment for entire families, including children, and enticed workers from Campobello, Grand Manan, Deer Island and other towns in Washington County. Rows of company houses sprang up and the company provided transportation to the factories. Until the late 19th century, youngsters of 11 years of age qualified for work. The children, unprotected by child labor laws until the 1930's, used sharp knives to remove the heads, tails and entrails of the fish; women sorted, added spices and packed the cans. When the factory whistle blew, all hands reported for work. Earnings were estimated by piece and the maximum earned a day was $3.00.

From 1799-1819 ship-building grew as part of Washington County. In 1804, the Frederick Augustus, a 329 ton vessel was built by Joseph Stevens. The name seems part of family history, although there is no clear connection. Records were few and often confusing because of the conditions for keeping them. Joyce Kinney has followed the history of shipping quite well through newspaper accounts but even Joyce admits the limitations of tracking the early years. She also writes in her book, *Real People Down East*, under the name Amos Boyd, that because of the lack of wireless or radio, many of the vessels and the men aboard them were lost at sea without a trace. Her commentary "…and when a vessel went down with its entire crew, their families never knew where or when they died. The sea is the world's largest cemetery."

Through newspaper articles, the fate of some of the many ships that went to sea is known as a history of tragic deaths, unbelievable survivals the loss of valuable cargo and the end of whole families. Some Captains brought their wives and infants aboard, some their eldest sons. And many never returned.

Early settlers included Acadians, forced to flee Nova Scotia, veterans of the American Revolution and others exiled from the provinces by the British. The results of the Revolution reverberated along the Maritimes and produced their special character.

Abstinence Down East Style

Maine was the home of the first Abstinence Society, founded in Portland in 1815 by Neal Dow, often called the "Father of Prohibition". This Maine Law remained in effect until the repeal of National Prohibition in 1934. Dow felt his cause as a Patriot and a Christian and by 1855, 12 additional states and 2 Canadian provinces enacted similar laws.

This must have been a hard sell as almost all residents of Maine felt alcohol was a necessity for health. There were no coffee breaks, Maine workers (and others) took alcohol for their "elevenses" in the morning and at 4:00 pm. As many began their day with a dram, the necessity was a reality. Even school children received this life giving draught at some point in the day, usually with breakfast. Backyard stills named "limbecs" were common and persistent. And it was just a short walk across the Canadian border if supplies grew scarce at home.

Enforcement of the law was a problem in most communities. The cost of identifying and destroying private property was not designed to fit most of the Maine mentality. "Oh-Be-Joyful" was the common name for spirits and the name spoke to a feeling acknowledged by those who survived heavy labor and Maine winters only with some external spirits. Joyce Kinney writes that the new laws irritated drinkers and the non-drinkers who wanted a option if they changed their minds. The overall attitude in town was marked by this law, a sense of joy was missing.

Despite Maine's own laws, rum had been a profitable trade item for years making fortunes for many. Most acknowledged that there was problem drinking but individual liberty to choose was a Maine standard. In Washington County, rum-runners did not usually carry guns, violence was rare (and unreported) and there were few secrets in the small populations of the area. Men found it worth defying the prohibition on liquor to feed their families.

The Volstead Act created more problems than it solved. By 1918, the federal government, laboring under the weight of enforcement, estimated a cost of $300,000,000 needed to adequately police the populace. By this time, the policy of prohibition had become a conservative cause as an issue of personal liberty.

The Volstead Act was not a popular one and as rum running had long been a practice along Maine's coast, there was a long history and a wealth of experience to evade the law enforcers. The Canadian border offered ways to smuggle as well, overland or down the Saint Croix River to Passamaquoddy Bay.

A break in routine happened on occasion when a loaded ship foundered on shore, depositing its content for the locals to salvage. On at least one wintry night, a truck became mired in heavy snow providing an open bar for those who found it. In all, the Maine climate, the proximity of legal spirits and the ease in making a living through carrying liquor from wet to dry areas ensured a constant supply was available if needed.

IV

Sarah Morang
and Nathaniel Macdonald

A patriarch of the MacDonald family was John Mac Donald, born in York, Maine in 1744, the son of John MacDonald and Susanna Young of Glencoe, Scotland, emigrants to the colonies. John's grandparents, yet another John MacDonald and his wife, Mary Robinson, came from Wicklow, Ireland. The times were hard in Ireland, harder still in Scotland. As precedent, the families packed up and moved to better lands.

John MacDonald of York, Maine raised a son, Nathaniel, who was born in Lubec in 1801 and he in turn married Sarah Morang of Lubec, Washington County, Maine in 1827. Eventually they settled in Eastport where their children were born. Sarah Morang became the wife of Nathaniel Mac Donald, more than ready to start a new family. Her parents were certainly part of the French culture, the MacDonalds added the Scots and Irish influence to the family tree.

The women who ran the households as well as setting off for factory work led of life of constant activity in those times but Sarah MacDonald did not have this dual workload. In addition, access to goods from England eased some of the chores designated as women's work on the frontier. Sarah and Nathaniel lived in an area of the country that had constant interchange with England and its goods. Nevertheless, tending kitchen gardens, making cheese, butter, beer and even cloth remained constant effort. A slaughtered pig required a sausage and bacon producer, and that was the housewife unless servants or older children were available. By 1850, most homes were equipped with stoves that gave the added benefit of heat. Unfortunately, the stoves required daily cleaning, blackening and a variety of cooking utensils. The simple meals cooked over an open fire gave way to dinners of soup, fish, boiled meats, roasted fowl, potatoes, turnips and celery. The housewife produced most of the food for her family. Sarah was busy.

Before 1890, poultry was purchased live to be killed, plucked and cooked. Fish came into the home with their scales intact, green coffee had to be roasted and ground, loaves of sugar to be pounded, flour sifted, and fruits seeded. Even raisins required preparation.

For Sarah and her daughters, housework was physical labor. Cooking was accomplished on a wood burning stove that required someones's full attention. Ashes must be removed, kindling and paper carefully arranged, flues adjusted and the fire lit. Steven Mintz continues his dissection of the stove in succinct wording. "Throughout the day, the stove had to be continually fed with new supplies of coal or wood—an average of fifty pounds a day. At least twice a day, the ash box had to be emptied, a task that required a woman to gather ashes and cinders in a grate and then dump them into a pan below. Altogether, a housewife spent four hours every day sifting ashes, adjusting dampers, lighting fires, carrying coal or wood, and rubbing the stove with thick black wax to keep it from rusting. The stove made edible food with much help from the designated cook but it also decorated the house and all in it with soot and smoke."

For those able to afford help, a cook could be had for $5 a week, a laundress for $3.50 and a cleaning woman for $1.50 a day. It was possible for some families to include an indentured servant to their household but it does not appear that the early Sarah had such help.

Clothing, then as always, was dictated by the society of the times. The custom dictated morning dress for inside wear. These dresses were made of fabrics easily washed, without decoration. Undergarments were of no nonsense material that could be boiled often and they were washed much more than the outer garments they were designed to protect. And there were corsets to be worn over the shift or chemise. The petticoat completed the under layers. Necklines were cut high and sleeves were long. The empire style with its high waist was well suited to pregnancy. Women did not cut their hair but parted in the middle and caught it in a bun in the back. Most wore mob-caps when home but if venturing out, hats were expected and frequently redecorated to extend their life of hard use. Shawls made of cashmere or muslin provided some warmth and a mantelet was another solution for cold climates. And ladies also carried reticules, parasols and fans when appropriate. Small wonder that Sarah was confined to her home.

Adults were living longer lives, Rosalie, the grandmother of Sarah Ann Mac Donald, lived to age 75, but early childhood deaths were common. Many young wives had the support of neighbors and family but many infants died suddenly without the services of physicians or medicine. Doctors came to the families with a little black bag—there were no complicated machines to tempt folks to bring their sick family members to wherever the Doctor resided. And they were few in number, often replaced by local herbalists who had a reputation for success when the patient survived or a rumor of black arts when the patient did not.

Children were especially vulnerable. It is amazing how many of Sarah Morang and Sarah Mac Donald's children lived to adulthood and even old age. Some changes came for the better in their lifetimes. Swaddling was replaced by loose clothing that could be washed and diapers were also washed rather than dried and returned to the baby. If soap products were bought or made, it was generally used for washing clothes, not people. The frequency of washing either was not remarkable for its regularity.

The MacDonald children were probably born with the services of a mid-wife although physicians were taking over from the women practitioners in the cities. As sterilization was not a common or well understood practice, many women died of puerperal fever, particularly in hospitals. The number of children born to a family continued to decline in the nineteenth century. It was clear that some kind of birth control was in use, for many, the application of Vaseline was considered the best method by some weary mothers. Literature abounded and the new mail system gave Americans access to pamphlets, devices and pills designed to produce abortions. The best deterrent was considered nursing, a not altogether effective choice. Sarah Ann Mac Donald, had some relief from the chores bourne by her mother, but she added new ones to even the score and a few more children as well.

Ten children to feed, nurse when ill and prepare for life is no small task. The bridegroom was 20 at the time of their marriage, Sarah five years younger. John Allen was the first child, born in 1827, the same year as Sarah's marriage to Nathaniel. The sequence of births was rapid—Olive came in 1828, Nathaniel Junior in 1830, Damietta in 1832, Francis, 1834, William, 1835, Moses in 1837, George in 1838, Sarah Ann in 1841, Marietta in 1843, Hannah in 1846 and Grace in 1848.

The separation indicates the belief in breast-feeding to prevent pregnancy. This did not appear to slow down the growth of the Mc Donald family. Sarah Mc Donald had reached the age of 40 when Grace was born. The family was complete.

The slow turn from Calvinism, that held that children were born sinful, replaced the pulpit message with the inspiring power of the mother to produce children who were good in every way. This was a heavy burden of the mothers with large families and little respite.

At age 46, Sarah's residence was listed in Charlotte County, New Brunswick, Canada. This is an interesting blip in the history of the family. Ties with Canada were strong but the children would have been too small to leave behind. The Civil War was years in the future so the mystery of this transfer is still open.

The 1851 Census of Canada East, Canada West, New Brunswick, and Nova Scotia records a McDaniel family that matches the MacDonalds of Lubec child for child. Campbello, Charlotte County New Brunswick was the registered home of Nathaniel McDonald, age 49, and his wife Sarah, age 46. The children with them were listed as follows: Olive, age 23; Damietta, 20; Francis, 17; Moses, 15; George, 14; Mariette, 9; Hannah, 5 and Sarah Ann, age 4. In all, ten of the family are on the census, and because Canada did not officially become a country until 1867, this is not the final word. Later census information is scant but it is clear that Frances, Moses and George would have been of an age to participate in the Union Army during the Civil War. They have not been found on any Maine records to date. Their recorded citizenship may have placed them in New Brunswick rather than Maine.

Sarah Mac Donald died in Eastport, Maine in 1892 at age 85. She was listed as widowed in the 1880 Eastport census which also noted "Relation of Head of House: Self". Nathaniel left his widow with many children and grandchildren in a place that was truly home. The years between need further research but Eastport was the home of Liddy Tibbetts Denbow and her husband, Nathaniel Denbow. It became the home of Sarah Morang and her daughter. The cemetery high on the hill overlooking Quoddy Bay is a testimonial to the presence of the family over many years. Water Street faces the bay in Eastport and it is now home to upscale restaurants alongside the traditional hardware and tackle stores. It is still an up-hill walk to Hillside Cemetery but the view is the same. Despite changes, no one who ever lived here could be lost.

V

Education in the 19th Century

As the Morang children grew up, they most surely learned to read with McGuffey texts. They learned phonics and each selection in their Reader was accompanied by questions to ensure comprehension, much as teachers do today. Lesson II in the First Eclectic Reader is as follows: "The cat. The mat. Is the cat on the mat? The cat is on the mat." Students were drilled on individual words and the sounds of e t I m and s with the correct diacritical marks clearly shown in the text to lead into sounding out new words. It is amazing how close Dr. Seuss is to William Holmes McGuffey in his approach, although the titles of lessons in the McGuffey Readers are quite a contrast.

In the Second Eclectic Reader, some of the titles are as follows: "Time To Get Up", "The Idle Boy Reformed", "The Kind Little Girl", "The Diligent Scholar" and "A Story About King Solomon." The books not only taught reading, they addressed the proper way of life for little girls and boys. They are still used by some home schoolers today.

Sarah would also study arithmetic, penmanship and elocution. Her formal education most probably ended in eighth grade but the lessons she learned about keeping house lasted much longer than that. Her character was well formed, she was literate and her cooking skills well practiced when she was ready to marry.

The Reverend William Holmes McGuffey began his own career as a "roving" teacher at the age of 14. He did go on to graduate from Washington & Jefferson College in 1826. He felt that children needed structured learning and so he planned a series of readers and published the first with Truman and Smith, a Cincinnati Publishing Company, in 1841. His Eclectic Readers presented the White, Anglo-Saxon, Protestant as the model American. Selections in the readers came from many sources. They were considered great literature and had huge influence on literary tastes. Between 1836 and 1960, 120 million copies of his Readers were sold making the Bible his only competition. A boxed set of the books can be purchased today from Amazon.com.

Schools

In a book compiled by William Henry Kilby, Eastport and Passamaquoddy, there is a chapter by Daniel Granger on early Eastport Schools. He speaks to the need for improvement of the public schools in Eastport which led to the construction of the Boynton School, dedicated on May 28, 1847. Private schools of excellence had been in place but the feeling in support of improving public schools grew quickly at mid-century. Land had been donated by Caleb Boynton, an original settler, and the school erected many years ago burned, providing space for the new high school.

A short local history is needed at this point. Prior to the Boynton High School, a small house on Water Street was operating as a school under a man named Greenwood. The house was 16 by 30 feet. It had two rooms: one was used as a tavern and the other functioned as a school. Mr. Greenwood owned and operated both establishments. His scholars often were interrupted by a call for service from the tavern—a call promptly answered by Mr. Greenwood. This released the students for "uncommon amusements" and those who attended the school remarked on their lack of learning and the pleasures outside of that activity.

When the town incorporated in 1798, a vote was taken for supporting schools. The answer was a clear "no". Votes were quickly passed on spending money for "powder, ball, flints, and camp-kettles" for the militia. Mr. Granger notes that the town was quick to perform its duty in relation to the defense of the town by a pronouncement of the grand jury of the town's neglect in providing for the purpose.

By 1799, the town of Eastport had been incorporated and it voted, at annual meeting, to raise one hundred dollars to support the schools. An act of the legislature in 1807 authorized the inhabitants of school districts to raise money in support of schools, supplementing the monies raised by the town. When Lubec and Eastport separated, money was in place to operate one "man's" school for a year and two women's schools as funding would permit. In 1812 when war with Great Britain was declared, the money appropriated for schools was diverted to assist the officers and privates stationed in town. From 1812 to 1815 there is a lack of records while the town was in possession of the British troops. The school-house had been requisitioned as a barracks, then returned to the district.

A strong effort was made in 1826 to erect a decent school-house. After a year of reports and positive votes Mr. Granger writes that he cannot fathom why such good intentions came to so "lame and impotent conclusion".

The spirit was willing, the results in a time when children as young as 11 were in the labor market, unsurprising. It can be noticed that private schools did exist in these times and produced students ready to attend college. Daniel Granger, for example, graduated from Bowdoin College in 1822, read law at the office of John and Ether Shepley in Saco, and was admitted to the bar of York County in 1829. He came to Eastport in 1833 and practiced law there until his death in 1854.

Books were there to be read when time permitted but there were other sources of education for the citizens of Maine. While mothers often were the primary lesson givers, they were not necessarily trained in motivational learning, multiple intelligences or higher level content. But mothers kept on learning too as lectures took on the form of entertainment.

One of the best of them all seems to be Robert Ingersoll. He took on many issues and was vehement of the subject of the secular base of the Constitution when it was challenged. But for this story, his support of women is notable. While both Elizabeth Cady Stanton and Margaret Sanger serenely accepted the inferiority of immigrants, Ingersoll championed them along with all the women. He rejected the idea that women were intellectually inferior to men, a belief held by almost all in his time. Ingersoll went far beyond the suffrage battle and asserted that birth control was a precondition for women's liberation from servitude. Jacoby writes that Ingersoll understood…. "that compulsory child-bearing was used by both the church and individual men to stymie any other aspirations that women might possess." He pressed for higher education for women to allow them full opportunity in whatever they wished to do. His thoughts on this issue are better served than many others as more women than men attend University in 2013 and more graduate as well.

As the century progressed, women became the largest consumers of books and magazines. Women wrote books and published articles and edited magazines. Many books were written by women and some reflect the sensitivity to issues unremarked by male authors. For example, in 1871, Elizabeth Stuart Phelps published *The Silent Partner*, a protests against factory conditions in New England and a plea for the better treatment of labor. Ten years later, Helen Hunt Jackson published *A Century Of Dishonor*, protesting the cruel treatment of the Indians by the United States Government.

Before the Civil War, a quarter of the teachers in Massachusetts were women. It was a task more formidable than keeping house for ten or more children as there were often sixty in a classroom, some older than the teacher. The teacher had to maintain discipline, teach a range of abilities and ages, and keep the schoolhouse warm enough to sustain life. It was a difficult job and it was said then that teachers wore out faster than any other class of people.

Those who had to work and couldn't teach might find employment in the textile mills of New England. Their pay was considerably less than their male counterparts: women received $2 to $3 a week, men were paid $12 for the same hours and the same work. A very few entered the professions as doctors, ministers, journalists, reformers and finally, as teachers.

For widows and orphans, the job market was slim and so the prospect of marriage held many advantages. For the same hours of drudgery and the pleasure of bearing and raising many children, women found some sort of economic shelter from a century where their rights were almost invisible.

Expansion of Education

Slowly but surely the principle of maintaining high schools at public expense became common practice. By 1857, students were encouraged to learn more advanced content. Algebra and even Latin were introduced. One Pennsylvania legislator did note that "the legislators never intended that Latin and Greek be taught at public expense". Today the demand is not great for either language. Although high schools began in the 1820's, the question of their existence was whether doors should be open to a select few or to all. In 1850 there were about 60 high schools in the United States with an enrollment of 359,949: in 1955, total enrollment reached 8,472,478. The purpose for their existence depended on whom you asked. Colleges saw them as prep schools, the state saw training grounds for citizenship and for parents it was the prolongation of education under the family roof. For those seeking equality, high schools were the people's college.

The President of Harvard University, James Walker, was enthused by the rise of high schools and saw better students arriving at college to the benefit of the whole system of public education. Harvard's faculty in 1857 boasted Louis Agassiz for zoology and geology; Oliver Wendell Holmes, anatomy and physiology; James Russell Lowell, Spanish and French Literature; Evangelinus A. Sophocles, Greek; and Charles W. Eliot, mathematics. In 1858, entry was dependent on the results of examinations in mathematics, history, geography, Latin and Greek.

In the same year, 447 students were enrolled in Yale University, 236 at the College of New Jersey, 274 at Indiana University, 207 at Brown and 160 at the University of Mississippi. Amherst, Bowdoin, Dartmouth, Rutgers, Wesleyan and Williams joined 13 other Universities educating the top students of the country.

After the Civil War, changes in industry, commerce, agriculture, politics, theology and science called for new techniques and skills. It is interesting that the high schools of the "frontier" in the west achieved a higher status faster than did those of the older states.

As time passed, there was a perception that students were not as smart as they used to be. Enrollment increased and many felt the faster the growth the poorer the quality of students. Not taken into account was the fact that the earlier schools enrolled the upper socio-economic classes. As time passed the most elite attended private prep schools reducing average ability determinations. Whether or not the average student was as smart as in the past, the result was needless sacrifices in requirements and the readiness to blame the quality of students rather than the educational process.

It was still a time when women in Universities were in scarce supply. By the 21st century, there are more women than men and more women graduate. The career ladder is still on shaky ground but the opportunities for women are in place. The appearance of women on the Supreme Court is leading towards better outcomes against gender discrimination, led at first by the indomitable Ruth Bader Ginsburg. Her staff, at one time, pointed out that the word sex was overused in her decisions prompting a change of verbiage to gender. And so it becomes an even more inclusive act of legislative change.

Changes to Come

By the mid 19th century, the new country spread to the Pacific Ocean, fought Mexico, built thousands of miles of canals, railroads, telegraph lines and forced the Indians from many of their traditional lands.

Popular democracy was ascendant and universal white male suffrage accomplished. The small beginnings of women's rights emerged and women founded their own literature. Sarah Morang of Lubec was part of these times and lived to see her grandchildren receive an education she had not.

While the Revolutionary War spurred the education of women to produce good citizens, there were many occupations in the early 19th century that required no book learning at all. In fact, one could manage without being able to read or compute. With the changes coming, the families of the Sarahs seem always interested in education for all their children, suitable to their times, perhaps, but sincerely held as evidenced by the stories of poetry read, lectures and plays attended and newspapers read each day. Eastport, though far from the major cities, held a geographic position that thrust its citizenry into foreign affairs more than most of the country.

The years between 1815 and 1848 changed the family and the country itself. It was a time of rapid development in transportation and communication: thousands of miles of canals and railroads were built, especially in the northern states, and this would have a heavy impact on the Civil War. Ocean liners and other vessels soon connected New York, Boston and Liverpool. In addition to the ability to move people, advances in telegraph lines opened communication to all parts of the nation. Under Jackson, the Indians were forced out of the south. In the 1840's, during the Presidency of James Polk, slavery was carried west.

For the new country, the defining event of the 19th century was the Civil War. The period of reconstruction was another devastating set-back to the formation of a more perfect union. Although the Pledge of Allegiance carries the words "One Nation…" full acceptance of the principle is still under debate in the 21st century. Into this environment came the war that split families, created incredible hardships for women and children of the north and south, and produced a generation where many men died or became disabled.

One change that would help to bring Civil War to the young country was on its way. The Missouri Compromise, signed by President Monroe on March 5, 1820, dedicated the great part of the Louisiana Purchase lands to freedom from slavery. The compromise admitted Missouri with slavery and the balance was maintained with the admission of Maine as a free state.

VI

The Nation

The new United States of America was feeling its way when the Morang family became residents of Lubec. Memories of political and economic problems in Nova Scotia and Quebec stayed fresh and the move southwards suited them on every point. The freedom from the increasingly onerous land owners in Canada gave their new home a special luster. A President who had been one of the Founding Fathers respected the farmer, carefully separated religion from government and was ready to ensure that secession was not an option. Long before the Civil War, Jefferson dealt with that possibility in the person of Aaron Burr. The background for future events was already moving into place at the turn of the century.

Some events merit attention. One such event was written of in a book by R. Kent Newmyer, Professor of History and an amazing authority on Constitutional Law. The name of Aaron Burr doesn't come up regularly in history books and its usual mention is negative. He was, in fact, a very unusual man and part of the nation's story. What families Down East thought of him is unknown but their independent nature may have given Aaron some sympathy.

The opening of the 19th century was celebrated by moving of the seat of government to Washington, D.C. When the electoral votes were counted in February 1801, a tie between Thomas Jefferson and Aaron Burr resulted. The House selected Jefferson and Burr became his vice-president. This seemed reasonable at the time but even today (or especially today) the second vote getter would not be the best choice for a Presidential team. The gridlock was noted and the 12th amendment to the Constitution corrected the problem in 1803: no longer would a tie be entertained. In the early 19th century, those governing the country were ready and able to tweak the Constitution when issues arose.

Jefferson believed in the people and he believed that agriculture was the foundation of the new country. He was careful not to equate religion and government. During his first term the United States Military Academy was opened on July 4th, 1802 at West Point; the United States completed the Louisiana Purchase; and the government supported the exploration of the Northwest Territories.

Although he had many goals in mind, in his first term Jefferson had a running battle with his Vice-President, Aaron Burr. The issues raised by this hostility still resonate.

What Is Treason?

The Trial of Aaron Burr, Jefferson's, Vice-President, gave indications of far reaching problems for the new country. Shortly after he left the office of Vice-President, Burr was tried for treason on the grounds of levying war for the purpose of separating the west from the Republic. The word "secession" was heard as early as 1807, putting forth the issue as a solution to problems of states' rights is still alive in the 21st century.

An overreaching of the executive office of the government was clear as President Thomas Jefferson actively worked to convict and execute Burr. In the book by R. Kent Newmyer, *The Treason Trial of Aaron Burr*, this particular event in history shows other issues to come. The separation of powers of the two branches government would be slowly defined as the Supreme Court took on additional status over the years. At the time, President Jefferson believed the elected representatives of the people had the final say in all matters, while Chief Justice Marshall believed that the law promulgated in the Constitution and interpreted by the Federal Courts should be above politics and the legislative branch of government. Two very different interpretations reverberate long after Jefferson's time in office.

Descriptions of the Trial itself defend Marshall's point. Newspapers of the time widely reported the proceedings, the riotous behavior of the crowds who attended them and the opinions of the leading figures in government and politics. The clear sentence of "guilty" given by the President before the trial, prejudged Burr and both newspapers and the average citizen assumed he was guilty. Richmond, Virginia, the location of the Trial became the center of public debate and all, both rich and poor, followed the Richmond Enquirer and the details it printed. The role of media, the separation of powers, the rule of public opinion, secession and politics became a framework to build on in later years.

Burr had a stormy career. His indictment for the killing of Alexander Hamilton in a duel was never tried in either New Jersey or New York where the papers were drawn. His acquittal of treason charges allowed him to go abroad but he returned to New York City in 1812 and died there.

In the midst of Burr's trial, the attack of the HMS Leopard on the Chesapeake occurred in Norfolk harbor in July 1807. The questions of impressment and blockades were finally answered in the War of 1812. The problems of the western territory were put on hold while the new nation addressed the issues of yet another war with Britain. Along the eastern seaboard and the maritimes, this was a call to action for the Atlantic Ocean was considered worth fighting for in any time. The ships of New England were of major importance, the men who sailed them became a burning issue as well.

The War of 1812

This was an unstable time Down East. During the lifetime of Jean Francoise and Rosalie Morang, the War of 1812 swept the area, bringing the European rivalries of Britain and France to North America once again. From the perspective of Quebec, the lack of sympathy from the newly formed United States for the struggles of the Mother country against the ambitions of Napoleon was a surprise. The seizure of American ships and removal of seamen suspected of desertion from the British navy seemed ample cause for Americans. And so Jefferson levied an embargo on British ships from American harbors.

How much lingering gratitude remained because of French support during the American Revolution is a question that would be answered. There was certainly a wish to fully acquire the last remnants of British America in order to tighten the borders of the new country. The final decision came with the election of James Madison who ran on a pledge of war with Britain.

Canada suffered most in the early days of the conflict as Britain instructed its military to ease off in hopes a compromise could be reached. It was a critical time in Europe with Napoleon at the peak of his powers and the British treasury running low. Many were facing the possible fall of Europe to Napoleon. War was declared on Britain by the United States on June 18, 1812. Jefferson predicted an easy victory. Henry Clay felt the Canadas were under American command. Canadians decried the intransigence of Americans who did not recognize the nobility of the British cause against the French.

Much of the fighting was centered in Upper Canada. The vast reaches of this land held a population of 300,000 men, women and children against an American population of 8,000,000. By winter, the campaign moved to Lower Canada where unrest over political interests caused the States to hope for support from French Canadians. (Lower

Canada received this designation as it was "lower" on the St. Lawrence River and populated by Catholics of French origin.) Once war was declared, all internal strife ended and Canada united in loyalty to the Assembly at York, now named Toronto.

The war moved on as winter ended and by 1813 French Canadians fought bravely for a country that gradually unified them all. The war continued on into 1814. Napoleon was in check for the moment and British soldiers, trained and experienced, were brought to Quebec. Rapid gains were made by the British forces during this time, bringing parts of the coast, the frontier of Maine and the entire region from Penobscot to St. Croix under British control.

The last battles of the war included the capture and burning of the city of Washington and an attempt to take New Orleans. On December 24, 1814, a treaty of peace was signed at Ghent. The defeat of Napoleon took away the profitable trade the new country amassed while the British–French conflict continued and a heavy war-tax hit New England hardest. Late in 1813, the British blockaded all ports south of New England. In April of 1814, New England's ports also felt the blockade. And there were secessionists in New England who dearly hoped for a chance to leave the United States. Nantucket made a separate peace with Britain, declared its neutrality and stopped paying taxes to the federal government. In British occupied Maine, some of the citizens claimed neutrality and some even swore an oath of allegiance to England. And there were those of French ancestry who sometimes took the brunt of anti-French sentiments.

To Historian J. Castell Hopkins and other Canadian scholars, this war was similar to the American Revolution as it consolidated Canadian ties with Britain for the entire population from the Great Lakes to the Atlantic coast. It definitively stopped the growth of Republicanism among the French of Lower Canada as it brought Canadians, both those of English and those of French heritage together in defense of their home.

In a new book, *The Civil War of 1812* (Knopf:2010) Alan Taylor writes that "No single cause can explain the declaration of war." He especially notes the allegiances and local vendettas along the Canadian/United States border are a story not fully told. The aftermath of war is a time to take stock. The Americans got not an inch of British territory and not much to add to the country's collective experience. The only consensus on victors comes from a clear acknowledgement that the Indian tribes were the true losers. The tribes along the frontier would soon be pushed out by waves of new settlers. Still, the American spirit was invigorated and Canadians were united as a nation. The world moved on. And the Morang family chose to become part of the New England culture.

VII

Home in Eastport

Eastport was defined by water. There were few places where you could not see the bay. The sun took it upstairs from lakes and rivers, it fell down as rain, hail and snow. Water provided jobs. It gave and it took away the wage earners regularly and was looked upon as a force of nature that had to be accepted. Across the expanse of the bay, you could see Canada, a reminder of the short distance between countries.

An Emery cousin, Joyce Kinney, still lives in Maine at the age of 89. She has written books about days past under the name of her dog, Amos Boyd. Her writings focus on the shipping news and folk stories: she is a remarkable woman. This project is indebted to Joyce because the past is so vivid in her mind. In 2012 she wrote as letter to explain that she did not have the energy to write as she used to do but her book has been well used in this one.

The rest of her response is quoted here with some expansions. "It's difficult to learn the way of life that was here in the nineteenth century. The isolation, except for Canadian associations, made lives very different from those in the rest of the country since people were closer in every way to the Maritime Provinces. For example, my mother, grandmother and great grandmother (the wife of Henry T. Emery) were all Canadian. Smuggling went both ways and when children needed medicine, food or clothing and it wasn't available on one side of the border or the other, smuggling was a necessity for survival. The watery border made it an easy choice.

Joyce added that the geography of the area affected everyone's daily life. No conversation or planning was complete without discussion of the range of the tides, the season, and the WEATHER! (caps were from cousin Joyce)

The home for the Emery children until the early 1880's was high on a hill overlooking Quoddy Bay. It still stands and the Bay is a town focal point. The house was built by Henry Tilton Emery and his wife, Mercy. Their portraits are in the Tides Museum. Their son, Frederick Augustus married Sarah Mc Donald. Frederick and his brother Robert left Eastport for N.Y.C. to start a shipping business. And so the link to Eastport ended although a visit there is like a visit home for the great-great grandchildren.

The Quoddy Tides reported the birth of each child. Townsfolk were amazed or chagrined depending on their personal opinions of the Emerys but it was a strong family and only well-wishers were encouraged to visit the new arrivals.

The Emery house was grey shingled with a front porch that had been enclosed for extra sleeping space. It sat high on Kendall Head, open to the elements in winter and the sun in summer. There was a bump-out window in the mansard roof, two chimneys for the fireplaces and not many neighbors. The house was large enough for the family and its heart was the kitchen. Homework was not an issue, no teacher would expect children to have spare time for that. School work belonged in school.

Lines and traps were mended at the table, dress patterns cut out, and fresh and pickled foods were prepared. Only at holiday times was the kitchen reserved for the culinary arts. Kitchen space was not gender biased, everything that happened there contributed to the survival of the family. The town of Eastport revolved around the fishing industry and the subsistence of every family did as well. But if the kitchen were the heart of a family home, the pier was the heart of the town

One of the first public spaces to greet the walker from the hills above Eastport was the pier. The pier at the foot of Water Street was not big but the bay offered refuge to the boats. Across from the pier the main street was lined with shops—mostly hardware and fishing equipment. When summer or winter storms came through, the salt spray hit the windows and it was rare to be able to see in or out. Horse drawn carts continuously moved from dock to factory in season but in the winter, sleighs carried the same loads up Water Street to the factories. Always, the waters around the city provided work. Sardine factories, factory camps, canning companies, clam and herring factory work, smoke houses and fishing could support a family, especially when any in the family could bring in a bit of money.

The dock did offer a wage to even young boys and all of them started earning in some part of the fishing fleet or in the factories. The boats were small and the men who brought them out to where the fish were had to be very strong, physically and mentally. At least the fish were there then and rules did not dictate how they could be caught.

Sarah MacDonald

The second Sarah, daughter of Sarah Morang and Nathaniel Mac Donald, was born in 1841. Her education was similar to that of her mother, the McGuffey Readers were ubiquitous in New England for their success in teaching reading and Protestant morality with a distinctly Calvinist base. Additional books were added to the series and other content matter as well.

The kitchen was an information center. When the Supreme Court struck down a long list of Progressive legislation that included child labor laws, union rights, minimum wage and the progressive income tax, the men of the house were angry. By allowing young children to work long hours, the commercial fleets could get around the standard wages of the town's men, thereby lowering their costs and increasing their competitive edge. The local paper reported the procedures faithfully, each day held a new issue to dissect. Judge Oliver Wendell Holmes despaired of the Court's over-reach and wrote, "A Constitution is not intended to embody a particular economic theory" in the overruling of a New York decision that the hours of work could be mandated.

While the men and boys worked in town, the women converted produce, fish, venison, squirrel and other game into salted, pickled and preserved forms that could carry them through the winter. The root cellar was stacked with bags of potatoes, beets, other vegetables, fruits and berries. Eggs slept in crocks of water until they were needed. The floor was earthen, the walls were built of stone and the cellar was the salvation of every family until spring. Some of the jobs were more pleasant than others and most girls looked ahead to passing chores onto their own children.

In *A Digital History of Housework in the 19th Century*, Steven Mintz writes of the problems of homes without running water. Carrying water in was heavy work but carrying out used water could be even worse. Laundry was labeled "the great domestic dread of the household" by 19th century housewives. Clothing and bedclothes were soaked overnight in tubs, scrubbed on washboards, boiled, rinsed twice, the second time with bluing, wrung, hung to dry and then pressed with heavy flatirons. Collars were starched.

Full hoop skirts began replacing a multitude of petticoats under women's clothes. The demand for whalebone made it a commodity for export but some hoops were made of steel to support the most elaborate dresses. The width of hooped skirts made exiting narrow doors a problem and the number of deaths attributed to ladies trapped in fires by their hoops increased each year.

The use of kerosene lamps added another chore to the housewives' burdens as the lanterns needed constant cleaning, filling and adjustments. In the cities, gaslight was becoming wide spread, in the country it took longer to install and to figure out who would be responsible. In addition to kerosene lamps, the housewife also had to deal with the intricacies of the Outhouse—an unpleasant job in any season.

The end of the century saw some relief. Carpet sweepers, electric irons and toasters appeared in stores and catalogues. Some processed foods were available—in the 1870's Franco-American provided canned meals and in the 1890's, Campbells brought forth condensed soups.

Mintz writes that the new labor saving devices did not shorten the housewives' duties as the rise in standards of cleanliness and childcare added hours of new responsibilities. An emphasis on health care made every wife and mother conscious of her role in maintaining a rosy cheeked family through her vigorous life as a homemaker.

Winters were long and cold. Summers were devoted to preparing for the coming winters. But this was not a life devoid of pleasure. Fishing was not a hobby but everyone made their own fun during the off time, painting, carving, hunting, cooking, sewing were all part of someone's choice. For Sarah, it was reading and poetry. She read some and wrote as she grew older. While others were occupied with their hands, she kept their minds active with her favorite authors. Shakespeare was one she loved and her leather bound volume was kept close. Her dream then was to see a play written by Shakespeare performed but it didn't seem likely to happen in Eastport. The Acme Theater featured shows, songs and singers, it was not a cultural desert but it chose to please the largest audience. One of the girls developed a repertoire of poetry she could recite easily. This was a skill nurtured in school where harried teachers set students to memorizing long sections of their favorite literature and in churches where memorization of large sections of the Bible were expected.

Imagine this. A grey shingled house looking down on rough waters from the front windows and the lights of the town a few miles away on the right side. To the left there was wind-swept hill and a rutted road led from the house to town. Inside the Emery house the family sat at table, each involved in their chore of the moment. And mother, with an eye on the weather for dramatic effect, recited

THE FIRST SNOW-FALL
by James Russell Lowell
"The snow had begun in the gloaming,
And busily all the night
Had been heaping field and highway
With a silence deep and white.

Every pine and fir and hemlock
Wore ermine too dear for an earl,
And the poorest twig on the elm-tree
Was ridged inch deep with pearl.

The poem carried on to its very sad ending and there were many damp eyes around the table. The words of the poet were affecting and so was the thought that tomorrow morning would bring all the difficulties of a snowy trip if any were at all possible from Kendall Head to town. The boys left to see to the horses, the table was cleared and everyone found their bed. In summer, this was not the end of the day, in winter it was the only choice. Winter was a time for poetry and reading but none were happy hibernators. The constant plea was to go to town although most activities were on hold. The schedule of events ahead held promise and the girls begged, cajoled and squirreled away fabrics, furs, lace and hat frames to build wardrobes for the new season. The girls kept count of the number of petticoats owned and the more the better although they added weight and bulk to their figures.

If winter comes, spring will follow. They were well, warm and fed. The flickering lights and fireplace were memories everyone of the family carried with them when they left Eastport for opportunity or settled in their own homes closer to the piers.

It was a long walk from Kendall Head into town but it was downhill. It was a tougher walk from the pier to the top of the hill overlooking the bay. As you trudged up the hill, the houses were bigger and grander. At the crest of the hill on the far right was the cemetery where most of the town folks were laid to rest when their time was over. Hillside Cemetery East, in the northern section of High Street, is the resting place of much Eastport heritage. Sailors and their families, both British and American soldiers and sailors, those in high positions and the ordinary folk of the town lie side by side. The oldest gravestone dates from 1800 and there are three tombs above ground. It is claimed to be a magnificent view from the mountain behind the cemetery.

The older girls made this walk from the time they could toddle until they made the trek alone, carrying a bunch of flowers for a family graves. The favorite destination was for a sister, Annie Louise, who died. Somehow it seemed more worth the journey to honor the little girl they never knew well. As they walked they imagined how the accident happened—it was horrendous in bright daylight and the girls tried never to think about it at night. The ever-present iron pot of water had tipped and spilled on the little girl standing near the stove for warmth. Everyone was careful not to stand near the iron pot even when acting as cook's helper.

In the mid-80's, the rivalry between the South End and the North End of town often led to fights and brawls. The poorest houses were closest to the water. When walking in and out of town it was smart to avoid the area at the end of Water Street. The Emery girls lived far from town and were unaware of the second life some of their fellow townsfolk led but their brothers were engaged in most town rivalries. The girls were told who they could meet with and which boys were off bounds. The family looked at the ramshackle homes with disgust. Buoys, lobster traps, tackle, broken bits of boats, oars and even bits of animals littered the yards. This was not a model for future life.

Perhaps the city did not produce Shakespeare but there were many celebrations. The 4th of July was huge, Memorial Day and June Day were highlights and the official end of winter. Old Home Week brought back many former residents and provided the town with tales of life outside of Maine. The circus came, and Eastport was on the Chautauqua circuit. Life was far from grim. Cold it was in the long winter but the celebrations of life were many in Eastport. As the family grew older, the entertainments of town became a focus, along with having the proper clothes and transportation that would save her good boots from the muddy paths.

In 1900, the number of Eastport residents reached 5,311. By the census of 2000, there were 1,640 still resident in the city. Racial diversity has never been a factor in city descriptions but there have always been households with no husband present, the life of the sea did not grant long lives to the men.

The close geographical ties to Canada resulted in extensive smuggling in the early 19th century and beyond. There was a cosmopolitan flair to Eastport because of the number of internationals passing through on business. These were also barred to the Emery girls and others in town who had parents to keep them at home when the outsiders came.

At that time, children went to school and left it when they could find something better to do. School was a seasonal activity, closely matched to the family's needs for survival.

The girls had an easier life—their exposure to the elements was more tempered but they had the difficult task of helping to feed many hungry people each and every day. The pot on the iron stove was always boiling. It began its life cycle as water and ended with the seasonal offerings and whatever fish came into the kitchen.

For most of the daughters it was the home they hoped to recreate when they came of age to marry. Several envisioned a marriage that would not be centered on the kitchen, however, but saw themselves far from Eastport in a location where the excitement of the theater and crowds of fashionable people was not in summer only. The sisters discussed the "locals", danced with them, walked with them and watched them go to work and home again.

The Maine days went by quickly in summer and as the older girls became accomplished housekeepers the younger picked up their chores and learned how to make cod fish cakes, fish soup and fish fritters. Most could sew, mend and remake a suit to fit. Nothing was wasted, ever. A favorite admonition to the next generation of children as they grew was "waste not, want not", a lesson learned in Maine. The girls found secret places to take personal sewing and reading, hidden from the eyes of mother. There was always a job to be done, an errand to run, or a neighbor to visit with and urgent requests for a cup of this or that. When one hiding place was found, another was located. It was this time that was devoted to creating a new hat or building a bustle of found material.

The events and celebrations in town went on despite the weather. Horses pulled sleighs in winter and carts in summer. Keeping one's appearance up to snuff while driving the five or so miles into town was difficult. The younger girls learned from their sisters how to fashion a scarf that kept hair in place and how to apply "lotions" that stopped the effects of sun and wind. Devotion to fashion was complete and as the sister's passed down clothing they all became expert in redesigning the old into the current mode. The girls would discuss the dress they noted at various activities, categorizing the outdated, the proper, the exciting and the over-the-top of each outfit. One flagrant example was dismissed as gussied up "like Mrs. Astor's pet horse".

Eastport, Maine was in a growth phase in the late 19th century, but the size of wages and the chances of advancement were slim. Sarah Ann and Frederick Emery had a large family and all were ambitious and so New York beckoned. Through several generations, the feeling that Eastport was truly home and New York only a footnote to life persisted. By the time Sarah Ann's great grandchildren heard the family history, New York seemed a small part of the years in Maine. The one son who stayed behind leaves little in the way of a legacy, his life as a weir fisherman may have suited him but history does not record his thoughts. The spell of Eastport is surely the memories, enhanced by distance, that give a special aura to the past.

Frederick Augustus Emery, born in 1838 found his bride, Sarah Mac Donald, in Eastport. Their marriage in 1861 marked the start of the Civil War as well as the beginning of their large family. Their marriage was hastened by Sarah's pregnancy and the two young people were quickly joined in matrimony the day before Frederick left for war.

The Emery House Kendall Head, Eastport, Maine

VIII

The Civil War

Eastport, Maine in the Civil War

The small State of Maine became a source of military manpower, supplies, ships, arms and support for the Union Army. Approximately 70,000 men from Maine were organized into 32 infantry, 2 cavalry regiments, 7 light Artillery batteries and 1 heavy artillery regiment. Hundreds of civilians served as nurses, doctors, relief workers, and agents at home and on the field of battle.

The people of Washington County voted overwhelmingly for Lincoln as President in 1860 but Joyce Kinney's search through the newspapers of the times shows the Machias Union and the paper published a dire prediction after the election. The Union's epitaph for the future citizens read "…Here lies a people, who, in striving to give liberty to the negro, lost their own freedom." As Kinney notes, not many agreed. One Pembroke lawyer who publically supported the Rebels was threatened with a coat of tar.

As Washington County's income primarily came from shipbuilding and the export of fish and lumber products, the men who sailed those ships were often far from home in the Caribbean or on the route to South America. Many had no idea that a civil war had begun. Other vessels arriving in Eastport brought news from the south.

Captains of merchant vessels were to keep to the outer edge of the Gulf Stream when heading to the West Indies in order to avoid capture of armed Confederate steamers. The Eastport Sentinel reported the capture of the brig Santa Clara only four days out from the West Indies. Both brig and cargo were destroyed.

An article found in the Eastport Sentinel is reported as written. "In January of 1863, the steamer Ariel, bound from New York for the Isthmus of Panama was captured by the Confederate raider Alabama, and after a few hours of detention, Captain Semmes of the Confederate steamer required the captain of the Ariel to give a bond of $225,000 to release the Ariel, payable three months after the Confederacy gained independence. The privateer confiscated all arms and ammunition, clothes and $8000 in U.S. Treasury notes." Many other ships were not as lucky. The brig Estelle was destroyed, its crew released in Havana. The brig Corris Ann from Macchias was burned, the barque Sallie Bonselle destroyed as were many other. In June alone, the rebel Tacony burned 10 vessels off the coast of Cape Cod. In all, 106 ships were destroyed at a value of $10,000,000. As the Confederate ships were powered by steam, their advantage over unarmed merchant sailing vessels was undisputed. The last ship lost to the Confederates was the schooner Alice Mowe, built in Eastport and at anchor in Cuba in 1865. This was mentioned in the Machias Union along with the other news of the day.

By February of 1863, English ship markets were filled with American ships for sale. Many of the ships were bought, renamed, sailed again under foreign flags and lost to history.

As the allegiance of people of the Maritimes were clouded by intermarriage and employment, ties continued between the U.S. ports and the British Maritimes throughout the war. For years men crossed the border at will looking for a better job or higher pay. Children in the same family might be born in either country and, as adults, support different sides in the war. Canadians were suspected of supplying Confederate cruisers, but, in fact some Americans were accused of the same passing of goods and information.

The Emery Family

Sarah Ann's brothers were of age by today's standards, perhaps not by those of the mid-19th century. From the New Brunswick Canada Census of 1851, the residency of Sarah and Nathaniel Mc Donald and family included Francis, Moses and George, ages 17, 15 and 14. By 1861, these boys would have been 27, 25, and 24. Three other boys seem to have stayed in Maine: John Allen, the oldest at 24 in 1851, Nathaniel, Jr. 21, and William, 16. There is no record of military service by any of the MacDonald men but an extensive search through military records has not been made.

Frederick Emery enlisted in the Maine Volunteers in August of 1861 and was mustered into the US army on September 22 of that same year. In between those two dates, Frederick Emery and Sarah MacDonald were married in St. Stephens New Brunswick, Canada on September 21st by the Reverend D. M. Kevenrie. Records show her father living in Campobello at the time and she may have been there with her family. Although Sarah had her mother, Sarah the first, to support her as she awaited her first child, the enlistment of Frederick in the 9th Maine Regiment was a difficult adjustment.

Although the political affiliation of the family is not recorded, the quick response of the Emery men to join the Union army suggests they were in the party of Lincoln. Party lines of the mid-19th century do not translate to the 21st but issues and actions surely do.

It was a rare occasion that brought news back to Eastport in the months after Frederick enlisted. Sarah's first baby was due and there were many times when she felt her husband would never return to see their child.

Information from the State of Maine Office of the Adjutant General summarizes the service of Frederick briefly in the records certified by Lt. Col, Armor, Assistant Adjutant General. Frederick enlisted in the 9th Regiment of Infantry Maine Volunteers on August 21st, 1861 and was mustered into the United States Service as a 2nd Lt. at Augusta, Maine on the 22 day of September, 1861. He was 22 year of age, 5 feet 8 ½" with blue eyes and brown hair. His occupation was listed as sailor.

The Ninth Maine Regiment left the State September 24th, 1861, and within a month they sailed from Fort Monroe to Hilton Head, South Carolina.

During that battle, 18 Union warships and 55 supporting craft under the leadership of Admiral S.E. DuPont bombarded the Confederate forces at Fort Walker and Fort Beauregard. After the 4 and ½ hour siege, General Thomas W. Sherman landed to establish the main Union blockade of the South Atlantic coast. A Marker, erected by the Hilton Head Island Historical Society, is located in Port Royal Plantation, Hilton Head, South Carolina.

In his time under General Sherman, Frederick contracted typhoid fever and blood poisoning, received an honorable discharge and left his regiment for home. His brother, Sabine, a Major in the same regiment, stayed on throughout the war. Sabine became a Colonel and led the assault of Strong's brigade on Fort Wagner.

Sabine Emery also volunteered. He was a graduate of Colby College and a former teacher with the persuasive ability to recruit men for the 9th Maine Volunteers.

The 9th Maine Regiment had its share of losses. In all, 10 Officers and 172 men were killed or mortally wounded. Even more telling is the listing of those who died of disease: 3 Officers and 236 men are in this category for a total of 421 deaths. Those who came home wounded and disabled were more than equal this number.

Frederick eventually became a 1st Lieutenant under the command of General William T. Sherman. While Sarah awaited his return, Frederick took part in the decisive battle of Port Royal on November 7, 1861. During that battle, 18 Union warships and 55 supporting craft under the leadership of Admiral S.E. DuPont bombarded the Confederate forces at Fort Walker and Fort Beauregard. After the 4 and ½ hour siege, General Thomas W. Sherman landed to establish the main Union blockade of the South Atlantic coast. A Marker, erected by the Hilton Head Island Historical Society, is located in Port Royal Plantation, Hilton Head, South Carolina.

The trip home by Frederick was one he never discussed with his family. He began the slow trip in October, 1862. It was soon winter and as he slowly retraced his steps north he met the new recruits moving south. The many ships of Washington County, Maine, were donated by their owners to aid the cause. The ships carried recruits south and the wounded north over the four years of battle.

For Frederick, the war seemed close even as he drew near home. There was no way for him to communicate with wife and family except through travelers heading north. His trust was not always well placed for they heard little over the year and some months he was away.

Although Sabine was still far from home, the return of Frederick was a cause of rejoicing for the two families. Eugenia had been born and was she there to greet her father. The next child was soon on the way. In 1963, Hilton was the first boy born of the union. All of Sarah Ann's children were born in Eastport.

Col. Sabine Emery 1835–1868

The Union and the Confederacy

More lives were lost in the Civil War than in all American wars before and after. As the cause of abolition gained momentum, the publication of Uncle Tom's Cabin by Harriet Beecher Stowe in 1852 brought the plight of slaves to the forefront. Just two years earlier, the Fugitive Slave Act had given southerners the right to hunt for runaway slaves in the northern states. This act aroused many in the north, but the book itself gave faces to the slaves as did the publication of pictures showing the results of beatings and the reality of shackled slaves at work in the cotton fields.

In *A Basic History of the United States*, Charles Beard includes a chapter titled Party Strife Over Government Control. The early comity prevailing during the "Virginia Dynasty" (Beard's punctuation) disappeared in Monroe's second term of office. For the first time, candidates courted the popular vote and giant events were held to showcase those vying for seats in Congress. John Quincy Adams won the Presidency and clearly stated his view of government as the entity responsible for improving the condition of the people through positive and reasonable measures. He was often opposed. Andrew Jackson replaced Adams as the champion of the people in both 1828 and 1832. A new party, the Whigs, grew largely in opposition to Jacksonian Democracy. Issues were vague during campaigns but one was most definitely freedom vs. slavery in the territories.

A new law passed in 1854 allowed territories entering the Union as states to choose slavery by popular vote. While Democrats opposed many governmental issues such as protective tariffs, national banks and sound currency, infrastructure improvements as unconstitutional, Whig orators, such as Daniel Webster, saw government empowerment to build the country fully Constitutional, citing precedents in action taken by George Washington and Alexander Hamilton, members of the convention of 1787.

Debates were studies in contrast, pitting the eternal nature of the Union against the idea of a collection of states that could choose to leave the union at any time. During this time, slavery was seen by more and more as a violation of human rights set forth in the Declaration of Independence. The Republican side-stepped the issue in part by ending the practice of slavery in the territories alone.

After the election of 1860, States began to secede. The Confederate States of the South, under the Presidency of Jefferson Davis, were well in place for the first battle of Bull Run in Manassas, Virginia.

At the start of the four-year war, Montgomery, Alabama was the capital of the Confederacy and although the South had no army, no central banking and little industry they had the power of a cause. It was estimated in the census that there were 4 million slaves in the south. They were not included in the military until the war was almost over and done. The North had a standing army of about 16,000, an industrial base and a strong aversion to slavery heightened by the runaway slave Act.

Families as well as the nation were divided in the years between 1861 and 1865. The end of armed conflict did not bring any kind of closure to those who fought. The Confederate flag still flies over state houses in parts of the United States and the basic issues of equality are still to be determined by all the people.

The three choices facing Abraham Lincoln after his inauguration in March 1861, were whether to allow the Confederacy to leave the Union, to find a compromise, or to preserve the Union through the army. In his inaugural address, Lincoln gave an appeal for problem solving within the limits of the Constitution. He declared at that time that the Union preceded the States and secession was unlawful. At no time did Lincoln challenge the question of slavery in states where it was legal. His message as clear:

as President, his oath was taken to "preserve, protect, and defend" the government of the United States.

Although the south was not solidly for secession, the large minority vote against it in Georgia, Alabama, Mississippi and Louisiana could not stop the steady move towards armed conflict. The division was so strong in Virginia that the western portion of the state withdrew and created West Virginia. Thousands of men from western North Carolina and the eastern parts of Kentucky and Tennessee, joined the Federal army. Secessionists in Missouri were finally driven out and the border states were no longer seen as part of the southern battle for independence from the Union.

"Buying Out"

The poorer women in northern states faced losing their men to war only if their economic class determined it to be so. The husbands and sons mustered into regiments through the first draft law of 1863 were mostly from poorer families. All men between 20 and 45 were subject to the draft. A man could "buy out" of the military requirement for $300, or, he could hire a substitute. Once a poor man was conscripted, his family lost all support for the soldier's pay was low and there were no allotments for families. Many women took jobs in the textile mills and munitions factories and the jobs were there for them. However, when the women replaced men, wages were slashed.

Middle-class northern women, rather than the government, gave some relief to these families. While feminists suspended their efforts during the war, they were responsible for both the draftees' families and the sick and wounded who returned home.

Those states having an economic base in agriculture were pitted against the states with manufacturing and agriculture. In addition, the government had the resources of the western territories. For the new nation, the cost of the war after pensions, interest on the Federal debt and the value of property destroyed was calculated to reach the amazing figure of $10,000,000,000.

From 1836 until the outbreak of the war, most banks were state operated and the value of their paper notes was increasingly at question. In 1863, Congress established a new banking system and placed it in the Treasury Department. Soon all currency was the product of the Federal government. This centralization of the economy was a necessity and a positive direction for the Union in the late 19th century. On August 2, 1861, Congress passed the first national Income Tax to pay for the war. That tax ended in 1872.

The Underground Railroad worked to help former slaves fleeing the south. Support for abolition was high in the north. Reports from the battlefield were few and far between, usually brought by the returning wounded. Much later, history documented the treatment of those Blacks who served in the Union Army. David Blight writes that the first regiment of the Louisiana Native Guards were mustered into service in late 1862— the first black regiment in the Union Army. The 2nd Regiment was sanctioned soon after and this regiment manned a prison for Confederate soldiers at Ship Island,

Massachusetts. The 21st century poet laureate of the U.S., Natasha Trethewey, wrote of one of that group in Native Guard, a Pulitzer Prize winning book of poetry. During their service, black regiments saw themselves fired on by both Union and Confederate forces. Union soldiers fired on them, and not the Confederates soldiers, at a battle near Pascagoula, Mississippi. Events are well recorded and clearly show that black troops were not accorded the rights of others in the field and blame can be placed on both of the combatants.

In that same year, in June, 1862, Mary Jane Patterson became the first African-American woman to graduate from college. Oberlin University in Ohio claims the honor. Mary Jane taught at the Philadelphia Institute for Colored Youth after receiving her degree and she later became Principal of a high school established for black youth in Washington, D.C.

Women took on heavy responsibilities during the war, including jobs exclusively the province of men. The mental equation of slavery and women's rights took strong hold and as women coped and grew, so did the movement for rights.

Womens' Rights During the War Years

These were the times that saw the beginnings of a middle class and a growing organization towards women's rights. As always, war accelerated the role of women in the greater society and ceded much of the power at home to them as well. Women who became involved in the abolition of slavery realized that, in effect, they were also slaves with few rights outside of the home. The start of the fight towards universal women's suffrage was begun soon after men achieved this right and the thrust of the movement came from early women led groups begun to protest slavery.

Education had slowly improved for girls after 1776 as it was felt women should be literate as mothers of the next citizens. The idea of them being educated to vote was not yet under consideration. By the mid-1830's, free public education was established for all children. The education of the nation's children had many goals: promotion of good morals and Protestant virtues, the "Americanization of foreigners", a more productive workforce, and the dilution of cultural and religious differences. The growth of an industrial society made the need for an educated work force a necessary priority.

After the Revolutionary War there was but one colony that permitted women to vote. It was New Jersey and that venue was closed in 1806 when a famous vote to decide the state capitol was decided in favor of the city of Newark over Elizabeth. The most interesting feature of this election was the number of votes which greatly exceeded the number of people. When the state legislature came to render a change in election procedures, reforms included an end to the female vote and women lost their opportunity to cast a ballot for a century.

Nevertheless, the fires were lit and in 1848 the first women's rights convention was called in Seneca Falls, NY. Thirty-two men and sixty-eight women signed a Declaration of Sentiments setting an agenda for the primary resolution calling for equal treatment of men and women and voting rights for all. Over 1,000 participated in the first National Women's Right Convention in 1850 and in 1869, after the Civil War ended, Susan B. Anthony and Elizabeth Cady Stanton organized the National Women's Suffrage Association whose only purpose was to gain the vote for women.

At last! Colorado became the first state to amend their constitution to grant women the right to vote. It was 1893, almost a century since New Jersey revoked that privilege. In 1896, long after the end of the Civil War, an effort was put forth by black women's clubs to form the National Association of Colored Women. Their cause mirrored that of their white sisters but the two groups worked as separate entities.

Civil Disobedience was one method used to gain attention and sympathy although it did not always garner the empathy of either men or women. Horror stories of the treatment of the early women suffragettes are now documentaries that disturb those who did not live through those years. The Fifthteenth Amendment assured the rights of male ex-slaves to vote, but not women.

World War I slowed the early progress but it also pushed women into the front of the labor market. After the war, the federal women's suffrage amendment, which had been introduced in Congress in 1878, was passed by the House and the Senate and sent to the states for ratification. On August 26, 1920, the 19th amendment to the Constitution was signed into law.

Margaret Sanger opened the first birth control clinic in Brooklyn, N.Y. in1916. Ten days later it was shut down and Sanger arrested. Undeterred, she opened another clinic in New York City in 1923.

As the 20th century began issues of improved wages and working conditions for women came to join the push for the vote. Shortly before the 19th amendment took effect, the Department of Labor added a Women's Bureau to collect data and monitor working conditions of women.

IX

Maine to New York

Sarah Ann McDonald and Frederick Augustus Emery raised a family that touched two centuries. The first of their eleven children was Eugenia, born in Eastport, Maine in 1862 and the line proceeded through Hilton, Beatrice, Edwin, Portia, Susie, Annie, Robert, Damietta, George, Sarah, and Everitt. The last of the children was born a New Yorker in 1884 and died in Centereach, Long Island in 1946 as a farmer who never once missed the life of the sea.

The Federal census of 1910 listed Frederick (71) and Sarah A. (69) as residents of their own home on the Middle Country Road, Brookhaven Township, Suffolk Co., NY and separated from Everett Emery by only one household. At that time, two of their boys were listed as stevedores. Everitt remained a farmer in Centereach, his final resting place in the local churchyard with his wife, Minnie.

Eugenia had traveled with her parents and siblings to Brooklyn, Kings County, New York when she was

18 years old. All of the children with the exception of Annie and Robert Sabine are present on the 1880 census as residents of Brooklyn. At that time, there was easy access from Brooklyn to lower Manhattan. The oldest boy, Hilton Frederick, made the move to Brooklyn at age 17, married Mary Ellen Clark in 1885 at age 22 and raised a daughter, Vergilia. He worked as a stevedore or longshoreman on the New York docks for many years.

Damietta Henrietta Emery married Harry N. Kellogg in 1895 when she was 20 years old and Portia Augusts was married at age 19 to George McClellan Davis in 1889. Records are sparse for the other girls but it appears that Annie was the small girl who died in a kitchen accident.

Pictures of Beatrice, or Beat, exist and show a small, slender woman with the fashionable dress of the times. Her later life was not happy but the family differs on why Beat more or less disappeared from the family circle. A rumor exists that she became pregnant and was institutionalized at a Long Island State Mental Hospital in King's Park.

Little is known of Susie but she did accompany the family on the move to Brooklyn.

Damietta followed the family tradition, raising a family of eight: three girls and five boys. She and Harry left New York for Milford, Connecticut in 1920 where the trail narrows down. Portia and George's three girls all lived in Brookhaven, their oldest, George, has no records.

Sarah Matilda was born in Eastport, the next to the last of the children. The family left Maine for Brooklyn, New York early in the 1880's so much of Sarah's childhood was not part of the Maine tradition but of the farm country of Brooklyn. Stories told by her family became a part of her heritage and Maine was never far from their thoughts. Eastport was not missed, but it did become an idealized part of family folklore.

The exodus of the family of Frederick Augustus and the second Sarah from Maine to Long Island coincides with the death of John. Henry Tilton Emery, father of Frederick, died in 1865 at the close of the Civil War.

For Sarah Ann, this was an enormous change and her youngest child was still a babe. Gone would be the support of relatives and friends but the positive side was the chance of keeping the family intact. Although the town was bustling, Sarah Ann and Frederick made a difficult decision, and soon the family from Maine was listed in the Brookhaven, New York census. Everitt, the last of eleven children, was born there in 1884. The Emery family that began as the Ameri's in France had resettled in rural Brookhaven, New York. The boys were able to work away from fish, fishing fleets, and canning factories of Eastport but life at the docks replaced Maine traditions. Frederick was 42 when the move was made.

By 1910 Frederick and Sarah had been married for 48 years, had 11 children with 8 of those still living. Their address on Middle Country Road, Brooklyn Township was next door to Everett Emery, their youngest child.

In 1915, Frederick Emery filed an application for an invalid pension at the age of 53, due to ill health traced back to the typhoid and blood poisoning contracted at Port Royal and Hilton Head during the Civil War. He was advised to resign by Colonel Rich after a surgeon agreed he would no longer be able to attend to his duties. He was honorably discharged at Port Royal, South Carolina on November 28, 1869. By the age of 53, the need for an invalid's pension was a necessity. He suffered from chronic catarrh, ague and failing eyesight at that time but had fathered a large family since his return from the war. Paper work from the Department of the Interior, Bureau of Pensions, makes clear "the disability is permanent and not the result of vicious habits, and that it incapacitates him from the performance of manual labor in such a degree as to render him unable to earn a support, and that this declaration is made for the purpose of being placed upon the pension roll, under the provisions of the Act of June 27, 1890. That he has not been employed in the military of naval service otherwise than as stated above." Further paperwork was requested to ensure the addition of Sarah Ann and their children to receive widow's/survivor's benefits if appropriate in the future

Eugenia had traveled with her parents and siblings to Brooklyn, Kings County, New York when she was 18 years old. All of the children with the exception of Annie and Robert Sabine are present on the 1880 census as residents of Brooklyn. At that time, there was easy access from Brooklyn to lower Manhattan and life was still very much connected to water.

Sarah Ann started her marriage pregnant and with her husband off to war. The tradition of family provided the care she needed until Frederick returned. He was never quite well again and much of the chores fell to her. She made the move to Long Island late in life, relocating the children and her ailing husband in order to be close to family.

Brookhaven, New York

The town of Brookhaven, first settled in 1655, is one of the ten towns in Suffolk county that is part of the New York metropolitan area. It stretches from the North Shore to the South Shore of Long Island, touching the Atlantic Ocean on one side and Long Island Sound on the other. A large part of Fire Island and the Great South Bay are in the town. To the east are Riverhead and Southampton and to the west are Smithtown and Islip.

There is a large rise named Bald Hill that marks the spot where the glacier forming Long Island finally stopped. Including water, it is the largest town in New York in total area.

During the Revolutionary War, The Battle of Long Island was fought along Kings County, now the Borough of Brooklyn in New York City. Many Loyalists settled in Long Island, especially in Hempstead but the island was a British stronghold until the end of the war. After the war, many Loyalists left for Upper Canada—many did not leave of their own volition.

In the 19th century, Long Island was mainly rural and agricultural. The advent of the steam ferry service allowed Wall Street magnates to get back to their Brooklyn homes in time for dinner. After the Civil War, street-car suburbs took over the outwash plain of central and southern Kings County.

In 1836 the beginnings of the Long Island Rail Road came as a combination ferry-rail route to Boston via Greenport. The line from the ferry terminal to Manhattan through Brooklyn to Jamaica in Queens was completed in

1844. At that time, railroads merged and grew, opening 50 stations in Nassau County and over 40 in Suffolk County assuring the suburbanization of the island.

Until the 1883 completion of the Brooklyn Bridge, the only connection of Long Island and the rest of the country was by boat. In all, seven bridges were constructed across the East River and tunnels followed as the population increased. On January 1, 1898, Kings County and parts of Queens were swept into "The City of Greater New York", abolishing all cities and towns within their borders.

The population of Brookhaven reached 8,595 people in 1850, significantly higher than the number of residents of Eastport. By 1910, that number had doubled. Brookhaven includes all or part of 50 hamlets, including Centerreach, Moriches, Lake Ronkonkoma and another Eastport.

Early in the 20th century, elevated and subway trains allowed masses of workers to commute to Manhattan from Queens and eastern Brooklyn. It was a comfortable life on Long Island for the many workers who had jobs in Manhattan. The Island became a retreat for the wealthy and the Long Island State Park Commission under Robert Moses crisscrossed the island with parkways and state parks. In the 1920's and 1930's, the island was a suburb and a place of mansions and recreation.

There are Emery's buried here too. Everitt and his wife Minnie found their resting place in Centereach and the churchyard doesn't look a lot different than it did when he died. The church is now on the register of historic places and the cemetery is well tended. Although the sense of past times is not quite as pervasive as it is in Eastport, it is a quiet reminder of the winding path taken by one family over several generations.

Brookhaven Congregational Church

The Docks

Since 1918, regularly scheduled Trans-Atlantic service between Liverpool and New York was in place. It sparked New York's rise to be the capital of global commerce. There were 771 miles of wharfs, and a constantly growing supply of cheap labor.

Mid-nineteenth century was a busy time at the docks. Irish Catholic immigrants dominated the waterfront and worked the waterfront precincts along both shores of Lower Manhattan. As Edwin G. Burrows and Mike Wallace wrote in Gotham, "on any given day five or six thousand of the longshoremen moved mountains of cargo off ships and around the port, roaming from pier to pier for the "shape-ups" at which native-born stevedores amassed work crews. The work was hard, poorly paid, and erratic. While waiting for ships to arrive or weather to clear, men hung around local saloons, took alternate jobs as teamsters, boatmen or brick makers, and relied on the earning of their wives and children.

Stevedores hired the men to load and unload ships. Those who worked the waterfront found exhaustion, danger and a lack of technological innovation until the mid-twentieth century. Only the strongest need apply as the longshoremen had only the most elementary inclines, pulleys and winches to move enormous weights. Families lived locally to allow quick response to in-coming ships. As unions began to form, they were strictly local entities governed by a sense of neighborhood prerogative.

Life along the waterfront in the Lower East and Lower West sides of Manhattan was dangerous. The New York Times reported in 1870 that the New York piers were "rotten structures, the abode of rats and hiding places of river thieves." Politics kept the waterfront from improving. The Tammany Hall boss, William M. Tweed, was finally jailed in 1872. By 1897 the municipal Department of Docks supervised the construction of municipally owned piers—some 700 feet long, on the riverfront between

Charles and Gansevoort Streets. Between 1904 and 1909 nearly thirty-five miles of new wharves materialized.

Into this chaotic situation came the Emery boys.

The name Cunard was well known on the Docks. Cunards came from Germany to Pennsylvania but were forced to move to Nova Scotia during the American Revolution. In 1839, Samuel Cunard, at the time a resident of Halifax, was part of the transatlantic shipping surge resulting from the development of steam navigation. The push was to facilitate intercontinental mail and bids were sought by the British government to take on that responsibility. By 1846, Cunard held a contract for a weekly mail service from New York City to England. While the Civil War disrupted ship-building, new companies in Liverpool ramped up technology and Cunard was considered an out-dated and rigid company.

Sam Cunard died in 1869. The new leader of the company began building Clydeside and the Cunard Line again held the speed records. In May 1915 the turbine driven Luisitania left for NYC. It was torpedoed and sunk 18 minutes later. The sinking of the Titanic was accidental, the Luisitania was purposefully sunk, ending a 75 year record of passenger safety claimed by the Cunard Line.

The loss of the Luisitania was one factor in the entry of the United States into World War I. The Cunard Line survived and built some of the fastest ships after the end of the First World War.

As a native Nova Scotian, Reginald Hughes was well acquainted with the Cunard Line and he became an employee when a young man in New York. His loss of that employment many years later was a cause of great anguish. In the years when union influence was making itself felt, it was necessary to align with the movement or suffer consequences.

The rise of unions was on the horizon. Men clearly saw the advantages of united stands for labor in all of the new industries. While action against unions was often harsh, the benefits outweighed the hazards of facing police, union busters, and lock-outs that became tools of employers. Women were not considered as part of this fight, in part because women of the times were expected to work until married but not after. This did not stop the practice of piece-work at home or deter women from trying to support families by themselves.

One tragic incident advanced the cause of women and union membership. The horrific nature of this factory fire brought public attention to focus on the plight of women workers in a way not previously possible.

The Triangle Shirtwaist Factory Fire

Life on the Docks of New York was difficult for men. Women had their own labor problems in those times, highlighted by the tragedy at the Triangle Shirtwaist Factory on Saturday, March 25, 1911. Sunday was the only day off for the women who worked there and the working week was ending when a fire broke out on the 8th floor of the Asch Building, located close to Washington Square Park.

The fire was over in half an hour. The top floors were locked and bodies were found huddled near those doors. Many jumped in order to try for survival. It was one of the largest losses of life the country had seen and it galvanized support for new safety laws in the factory system.,

At the close of the efforts to reach survivors, 146 bodies were left in the building and on the grounds around it. All but 23 were women. Later, survivors testified that the doors were locked—a practice done by the factory owners to ensure promptness (doors were locked at the time of check-in), to prevent shirtwaists disappearing (all leave-takers were searched before going home), and to prevent workers from joining protests. It was a common strategy used by employers in NYC factories of that period.

The protests began to address the issues of sanitation and fair wages. The mostly Jewish women who worked in the factories were paid 35 cents an hour while girls in Union shops earned 60 cents. In part, this discrepancy ensured the longer working hours of the girls at the Triangle Factory. Experienced workers were used to train newcomers, mostly Italian, and then fired. It was an industry ripe for reform and it took a disaster to focus attention on the injustices suffered by poor women new to the city and the country they heard had streets paved with gold.

One result of the deaths of these young women was the strengthening of the ILGWU. The International Ladies' Garment Workers' Union, founded in 1900, had a membership of a few thousand and most were women. The union fought for better working conditions, wages and hours and after the Triangle Shirtwaist Factory fire, for safety standards in the workplace. Membership increased at this time and by 1969, the union had over 450,000 on its lists. The ILG has merged with other unions but its early strength brought about many changes that improved the working conditions of mainly immigrant women in the textile industry.

The fire in the Triangle Shirtwaist factory gave impetus to the call for improvement in the textile industry as it put a face on the women who were the workers. It is unfortunate that the leadership was almost exclusively male for many years.

Unions were growing as "industrial democracy" became a cause for many, both rich and poor. The morality of the country was aroused by the deaths of so many hard-working young woman. They are remembered annually at the site of the fire—it is an event in US history that will not be forgotten.

X

Sarah Emery Hughes

I n 1880, Sarah Matilda Emery was born to a family with nine children. Even in Eastport, Maine, this was an event to arouse comment. Most of the children were named to reflect their French background but Sarah's mother had exhausted her string of feminine names and ended the female line with her own.

The sequence of birth produced the list of responsibilities associated with family membership. As the baby, Sadie didn't assume the duties her elder sisters managed daily and she shared the role of the large, black, mixed breed dog as family pet. As the sisters left to begin new families, their duties eventually became hers. As Sarah grew she showed a love of theater and poetry.

One of her favorite poems was learnt by heart and her grand-children heard it with little comprehension many years later. Sadie had a love of poetry and a sly wit that appreciated Holmes. Her own poems show the same flow of understanding for the foibles of mankind. The plain brown stone replaced the shingle of Eastport in Sarah's life and she remembered none of her Eastport beginnings except through her mother's stories. Her choices in poetry were more urban than country although the family lived in farmland. The city was always a special place for Sarah the Third.

"Man wants but little here below"

by Oliver Wendell Holmes
Little I ask; my wants are few;
I only wish a hut of stone,
(A very plain brown stone will do,)
That I may call my own;
And close at hand is such a one,
In yonder street that fronts the sun.

Plain food is quite enough for me;
Three courses are as good as ten;
If Nature can subsist on three,
Thank Heaven for three. Amen!
I always thought cold victual nice;
My choice would be vanilla-ice.

I care not much for gold or land:-
Give me a mortgage here and there,-
Some good bank-stock, some note of hand,
Or trifling railroad share,
I only ask that Fortune send
A little more than I shall spend.

Honors are silly toys, I know,
And titles are but empty names;
I would, perhaps, be Plenipo,--
  But only near St. James;
I'm very sure I should not care
To fill our Gubernator's chair.

Jewels are baubles; 'tis a sin
To care for such unfruitful things;
One good-sized diamond in a pin,--
  Some, not so large, in rings,--
  A ruby, and a pearl, or so,
Will do for me—I laugh at show.

And the poem continues in humble and self-sacrificing
fashion with tongue firmly in cheek. Sarah Matilda could
recite it all from memory. She had a keen sense of humor
all her life and often used her own poetry to express
opinions. Poetry, the theater, and later, the movies affected
her life and she stayed interested until her old age. Clearly,
her real treasure was family.

The Emery's did not stay long in Eastport after Sadie's
birth. By 1900, their official residence was in Brookhaven
Township, Election District 6, Suffolk, N.Y. Sarah Matilda
might have Maine in her blood but she grew up outside
of one of the largest cities in the world.

There were choices in New York. The docks were
accessible and land for farming was rocky but available.
The finest Brownstone homes were not those Sadie
dwelled in but she was always well aware of how others
lived in the city.

Sadie's brother, Hilton, was a stevedore. He brought a guest one summer. It was just a visit to break the hard work of the docks. His friend had come down from Nova Scotia and was a seaman, not a dock-worker. His name was Reginald Corbitt Hughes, a fulsome name for a handsome man. Sadie was immediately taken with his sense of presence, his past experiences, his love of music and his career at sea. Their courtship spanned several years and Reg was at sea for most of them.

Sadie seemed the spark in all-family decisions and Reg became the source of light and laughter. Born in Annapolis Royale, Nova Scotia in 1880, his life at sea started early. He and his brother George emigrated to the US in 1892 and lived together in Brooklyn. George was listed as a purser on the U.S. census records, Reg is written down as mariner.

Near the turn of the century he sailed to Panama, went through the Suez Canal with the Howard Gould yacht, worked on a sealer in Alaska and Japan in the late 1890's and sailed on the Red D Line to the Dutch West Indies. Reg became a naturalized citizen of the US in 1900.

He began as a seaman but when his health declined and his family burgeoned, he stayed on the docks as a stevedore and then a timekeeper for Cunard.

This letter came to light once again in 2012. It is included to give a clearer picture of the man Sadie chose to marry. While she worried about the little things she had to report, his letter seems another world entirely, yet his mastery of the places he saw was exceptional. The New York Tribune reported on the trip, but from the point of view of Howard Gould and his guests who boarded his steam powered yacht Niagara. The article in the Tribune was especially focussed on the cost of the yacht and the cost of its maintenance. After exhausting the details of a millionaire's purse they described the trip much as Reginald did in his letter to Sadie. A photographer was on board and so a record of the tombs, monuments and temples they visited was recorded well. Howard's favorites were Luxor and Karnak. Photos show a string of well dressed ladies and gentlemen walking into famous sites. The yacht anchored at the mouth of the Nile for three weeks while the party used a smaller hire to visit sites along the Nile. They left Alexandria in February, made a short stop in Gibraltar for coal, a brief visit to the Canary Islands and, in 25 days were back in New York Harbor.

★ A Letter ★

On January 19, 1903, Reginald wrote to Sadie from Alexandria, Egypt. He encouraged her to write about the "little things" as everything was of interest to him and he was so lonesome. In his letter, he sums up the trip to date. The following is the original letter, intact.

"Well I will give you my adventures up to date. We left Bermuda Dec. 15th and for 10 days saw nothing but sea and sky but we had fine weather no wind only an occasional rain squall At daylight on Christmas morning we sighted Maderia Islands and a few hours later dropped anchor off the town of Funchal. It is a curious looking town sitting on the side of a mountain 6,000 feet high. It is a very old place settled in 1740 by the Portuguese…. The people were have a fine time celebrating Xmas, shooting off guns, fire crackers, rockets etc. They have no horses or carriages here but instead a yolk of oxen or bullocks hitched to a (what do you think?) a regular old fashioned wood sled with a canopy over the top of it. The streets are so steep that his rig works better than wheels and they use two drivers, one ahead and one berthing each one with whip. Never had a real good sleigh ride without any snow before. There is a railway to the top of the mountain and you can take a toboggan slide for 2,000 feet. Madeira was a pretty nice place.

We left there on December 27th bound for Gibraltar. The rock of Gibraltar is something fine to look at a great rock rising right out of the water. We only stayed there a few hours and left for Algiers. We arrived there on New Years Day. Algiers is certainly alright. I liked it better than any place I have yet been in, It belongs to the French. They conquered the country in 1830. You remember the play we saw in New York last year, It was great fun watching the Arabs and the different nationalities. The King of Dahomey was in town and he was a little blacker than the others. Take it altogether, it was a great looking crowd. We had a fine time among the French people. We left there on January 4th bound for Malta and followed the African coast along, passing Tunis and other cities. Tuesday the 6th we arrived in Malta.

This is a famous old place. It has been known ever since the crusades. To look at it from the water it reminds one of a piece of scenery one sees on the stage. All castles, forts and odd looking houses and streets. There was a powerful English fleet here besides lots of English soldiers. Ashoure, the women here wear a curious sort of a bonnet, something like the sun bonnets worn in the country. Under the streets of the town are great warehouses for holding provisions in case of war. Soldiers and civilians number close on 200,000 and there is enough materials to last 7 years. Every year they take out 1/7 of the supplies and use it up, but they always replace it with a fresh lot.

We left Malta on the 8th, bound for Alexandria and arrived here on the 10th. 31 days from New York, a long sail was it not? I won't say anything about Egypt in this letter as I mean to write you again before we leave and we will lay here until the last of February. I might say that by looking out of the port hold in my room I can see the Chedives Palace and Harem where he keeps 150 wives. He certainly has a large number of better half's. Now you can't say a word about sailors, can you? The weather is cold here, especially the nights. The Arabs are walking around with half their bedclothes piled on their backs besides their ordinary clothes.

Well I must say good bye, little girl, hope to see you next April if all goes well. Write as as soon as you get this. Yours very sincerely, Reg, C, Hughes"

Reginald Corbitt Hughes

Mary Ellen Corbitt Hughes West

Marjorie Hughes at One Year

A last letter reached Miss Sadie Emery in February 1904 at 522 Chauncey Street, Brooklyn. They determined to marry.

Weddings required a trousseau. The next winter's sewing was of linens to start a new home and clothes for at least a year. The one black silk would be suitable for New York outings but the women were not quite sure what young wives would wear on a daily basis. Reg and her brother were asked questions on current fashions but their answers were not helpful. The length of skirts seemed the detail they had noted but not much else. Sadie fretted and fussed. She knew she would be judged by her wardrobe. Magazines came into the house and a new corset was purchased to help with fittings. At $1.50, the corset cost more than some of the dresses. Sadie's mother chose high necks, some lace and a modest bustle. Sadie held out for Bertha collars, velvet suits and one new silk for gala events. Mother picked black wool broadcloth, Sadie slipped in a silk taffeta. Whatever the neckline, the sleeves contained a large amount of the total fabric used. There was no sewing machine in the house and many fingers were pricked in making the clothes.

When they finally decided on a date, no elaborate wedding took place. Like her mother, Sadie and Reg eloped. They were married on March 28, 1904 on Fleet Street in Brooklyn, NY. They found a place to stay in Manhattan to give Sadie a home closer to the docks when her new husband was off at sea.

Sadie's had a new best friend, in New York. Mary Ellen Corbitt Hughes, her mother-in-law, was more than ready to show her the town. The gossip was that Mary Ellen was a real gad-about. It is a tribute to her that she was as lively as a grandmother could be. Her life married to a seaman was never easy in Nova Scotia and her first husband, Reg's father, died at sea. Eventually, Mary Ellen became Grandma West as she remarried.

Mary Ellen had a love of theater and the means to share the delight with her son's wife. Grandma was a lively and acceptable companion for the young Sadie. They went out often and saw the races, musicals, plays and variety shows that were part of the life style of New York. It was a time of magic. Mary Ellen did not bake cookies:

she was a party girl. She quickly taught Sadie how to stay sober by dumping her drinks in the potted plants. Each time Reg came to port, he was included in the outings. He loved Enrico Caruso and slowly gathered a collection of his records. When they counted them while packing to move, he possessed fifty of the 290 Caruso eventually pressed. And one special night they went to the Met to hear him in person.

Their first child was born in 1907. It was a change in schedule for Sadie but the baby was welcome. They would have a family like the one she had heard described by her mother; large, lively and devoted to their parents. After Marjorie and her two brothers joined the family, the focus changed from the excitement of the theater to the realities. No disposable diapers, no washing machines, no take-out. The winters seemed long but there was no lack of chores and little help. Grocery shopping was easy: laundry was not.

When Marjorie became old enough to take charge of the boys, the theater became possible again. At the age if eight, Marjorie was often in charge of her younger brothers. She was not a pampered baby but a girl with many duties. The daily run to the neighborhood grocery store was made by Marjorie. She was always fearful that the shopkeeper might demand money rather than write down the charge in his book. One day she returned without the groceries, tears streaming. "What happened—did you lose the list—did you lose the money?" Sadie was almost crying herself. "Mother, a man killed a horse," Marjorie sobbed. "The horse was just lying down and the man came with a gun…" "Alright, Marjorie, stop right now.

The horse broke its leg and horses that can't walk must go to sleep. It will happen again but now you know why. Where is the list? And the money? You go back to the store right away, I need those things for supper." Marjorie left, a sobbing, miserable little girl. She never forgot the horse but Sadie had other worries.

Sadie often requested a trip to the drug store to buy Jergens face cream, appearance was important to her and this was her brand. The children were beauties—two with her dark hair and one distinctly red headed like his father. Pride in appearance was a family characteristic for Sadie and she carefully presented herself and children as models of perfection. An early picture of Marjorie shows a little girl in a huge hat, dressed in white flounced dress, belted by a wide sash, white stockings and black boots. She looks pensive but aware of her finery. For the rest of her life, just like her mother, a hat was an essential part of any outfit.

Kenneth and Hilton were next in line, then Doris and in 1916, George Alexander. All born in Brooklyn and the spell of New York City never left Marjorie and George. The family moved from Long Island to an area close to 18th Street in the city where Reg could get to work on time. Transportation from Long Island was difficult and lengthy at best. As the boys grew up the neighborhood grew as well and Kenneth and Hilton were having problems with "John's Gang" the beginnings of a city trend.

In 1910 the US Census reported Reginald living at 434 36th Street in Brooklyn, NY and his occupation was seaman. Their residence was in Brooklyn Ward 8, Kings, N.Y. Sadie's black hair was now coiled in a twist, blue eyes ready to observe and follow new behaviors. There were several moves after that initial jump—Yonkers in 1915 and the Manhattan Assembly District in N.Y. N.Y. by 1920. Somewhere between that residence and Lyndhurst, decisions were made to find another home, safer for the children and with room for a garden. It was a bittersweet decision but even Sadie faced the inevitable change in her life through complete immersion in the family they were building.

The commute to the piers from Long Island was a long process but the move to the city had posed challenges for the children. They began by looking at ways to get Reg in to the docks. That meant access by rail. Surrounding towns were checked for trains and housing and the final choice was Lyndhurst, New Jersey. For Sadie, home would always be where Reg was. School was not an issue, she knew the children would be fine. Perhaps the boys and girls they met in New Jersey would be less aggressive.

XI

Moving On

Lyndhurst, New Jersey

It was time to move on. Reg was still working on the docks but the two researched rail lines and found Lyndhurst would be an easy commute. By now, it was much easier than the trip from Long Island.

Marjorie helped with the packing on the move to Lyndhurst. She would not miss her school and hoped for one where the children were dressed nicely, clean and eager to learn. Her brothers were a constant worry, just knowing where they were was a full time job. Sadie would ask frequently, "Where are the boys?" and Marjorie would quickly answer "In the schoolyard playing". Maybe not. It was the answer best accepted and used almost always. But then she would leave on an errand and search them out, herding them home with determination.

The day for the move came and the family took what they could carry to the train station, managed to find seats and left the city for the country. So much was left behind for Sadie but Reg was home each night. And the house would hold the five children and maybe more. The Lyndhurst house was half-way down a hill that started at Main Street and ended at the Passaic river. There was moving water in walking distance, a train for trips into the city, grocery stores, a garden and a school. This would be home for many years.

The house at 209 Lake Avenue was right in all ways. The trips to the city continued and Sadie continued to travel in for movies and shows, later taking the older children with her. Louise remembers a trip to the Hippodrome to see Douglas Fairbanks. On another trip to see Tobacco Road Louise was left at home and she remembers that as well.

An accident stopped these excursions. Sadie fell from the attic ladder, twisting and breaking an ankle that never properly healed.

The family settled in. Two large bedrooms served the children and a huge bedroom with dressing room and bath was set aside for their parents. The major part of each day took place in the kitchen. Food for the family was the first thought on rising and the last when dishes were done and the stove closed down for the night. Those years were happy enough to produce another child, born in 1923.

The house had a large dining-room, separated from the living room by an arched panel. Sadie was a person who enjoyed seeing it full. Louise recalls a dinner party of 12—all related through Uncle Ev although he wasn't present at the time. Louise remembered the names of those introduced nearly 30 years later: Agnes, Julia, Vergillia (who she decided looked French) and on the other side of the table, Evelyn, Donald and someone who may have been a husband. Kenneth, Hilton, Doris and George were all present. It was a happy day.

A garden was the focus of the yard. It provided a place for Reg to think, food for the table in summer and in winter, rows of glass containers with vegetables grown behind the garage and preserved in the huge kitchen. Sadie's time was spent with food and the table was always full. Pickled beets, red cabbage, beans and stewed tomatoes were the staples. Reg often brought something home from the docks when a net "accidentally" broke and showered the workers with cans of food. It was rare for nets to break with machine parts. He also brought home bags of crabs or lobsters, freeing them for a last run around the feet of his children. He was tall with red hair and a constant smile. He and Sadie were a striking couple at the turn of the century, even after the sixth child came along. It was a match made for love but the head of the household, the decider, the arbiter was always Sadie.

The change of life style was more related to the number of children than the address. This was surely less than her mother had coped with and Sadie wondered why it took her seven days a week to feed and clothe only six children. An Emery relative was contacted in Centerreach, Long Island and for the first time, the children left home to "vacation" with an uncle and aunt on their farm. They ate well, rode the donkey and horse, played freely and came home sunburnt and happy. With only two at home those summers, Sadie felt young again. Her access to fashion was through pattern books instead of viewing other women at the theater. Her skill at sewing was amazing after they took the plunge and bought a treadle operated sewing machine.

Reg lost his job as Time Keeper with Cunard. The company decided on extensive cost cutting, firing many of those close to retirement. Louise remembers her father sitting on the porch steps, despondent and worried. But he did find another job in New Jersey and worked until his 65th year. The loss of his pension was a huge burden to bear. He had not joined a Union and had no recourse. The New Jersey job saw him and the family through those times.

209 Lake Avenue, Lyndhurst, N.J.

Kenneth, George, Marjorie, Doris
and Hilton Hughes

Marjorie Hughes

Doris Hughes

Louise Hughes

An Event that Impacted Later Times:
The Dreyfus Case

In France, the constitution of 1875 established the Third Republic and provided universal manhood suffrage and political rights to the people. By 1880, it was considered secure. In the last two decades of the 19th century, scandals were numerous. The most serious was the Dreyfus case.

Alfred Dreyfus, a Jewish officer in the French army, was accused of selling military secrets to a foreign nation. The case developed into a bloodless civil war fought by those against the Republic, the army, the church, and the royalists as symbolized by Dreyfus. The Dreyfusards were mainly the intellectuals and socialists.

Donald E. Wilkes, Jr. wrote, "it is Monday, October 15, 1894, in Paris, France. The Dreyfus case—the most notorious frame-up of the 19th century, one of the most incredible episodes in criminal jurisprudence, and an important chapter in the history of anti–Semitism, is about to commence." Dreyfus was arrested on a charge of treason that morning. He protested but was confined to a military prison, tried behind closed doors on the basis of forged documents, and sentenced to life imprisonment. He was formally degraded and expelled from the army at a military ceremony watched by a mob screaming ani–Semitic epithets. He spent four years in solitary confinement on Devil's Island off the coast of South America.

Those who fought for the truth suffered as well. Lt. Colonel Georges Picquart became head of the French armies intelligence section and soon discovered the true writer of the incriminating letter. It was written by an infantry officer, Commandant Esterhazy. For his role in finding this information, Picquart was sent far from France, disciplined, imprisoned and expelled from the army.

Emile Zola, who published an article titled *J'accuse* to bring out the miscarriage of justice was convicted of criminal libel and spent a year of exile in England. When L'Aurore, the newspaper that published the article, was on the streets of Paris, mobs demonstrated, burnt Zola in effigy and continued on to assault his home. Even worse, "mobs rioted and sacked Jewish quarters in most of the larger towns and cities throughout France, while in Algiers, Jews were killed and their shops destroyed."

Those who stood with Dreyfus were primarily the intellectuals of France: Marcel Proust, Anatole France, Octave Mirabeau, Emile Duclauz, Pissaro, Monet and other artists, writers and thinkers. Nevertheless, Zola had to flee to London, fearing for his life.

A civilian court finally overturned Dreyfus' conviction in 1899 and he was returned to France where a retrial found him guilty, once again convicted of treason by a military tribunal. A world-wide uproar finally resulted in a pardon from the President of France. In 1906 Dreyfus was declared innocent by the highest court in France, honorably restored to the French army and awarded the medal of the Legion of Honor.

The generals and officers who persecuted Dreyfus were never punished. Alfred Dreyfus served as a Commandant in combat during World War I. He died in 1935. His life was honorable throughout.

World War I and Changing Times

In the period before the first World War, Europe's population doubled, the spread of public schools almost erased illiteracy, literature was available to all and science provided the telephone, telegraph, the locomotive, steam boats, and gas illumination. Governments were more open to the voice of the people and laws were passed to protect workers as the expansion of the vote addressed middle and lower class concerns.

Globalization was emerging as the interdependence of all nations showed the advantages of a world community. Yet Wallbank and Taylor in *Civilization: Past and Present,* wrote in 1949, "If men could be said to have reached a position just lower than the angels in their intellectual and scientific attainments, their tactics in international relations fell considerably short of the mark."

The cause of WW I can be attributed in part to the insecurity of European nations whose fears promoted secret alliances and an armaments race. This, in turn, moved towards a struggle for markets, raw materials and colonies. When war was declared, the United States hung back. The sinking of Cunard's Luisitania in 1915 did give a more immediate reason for the U.S. to join forces with Britain and her allies.

For the purposes of legacies, the ending of the war is as important as the horrors of its perpetration. This war took the lives of a generation of young men, bankrupted governments and caused the fall of old monarchies. Starvation took hold on the entire continent and many regions were in chaos. The League of Nations, promoted and defended by the idealism of President Woodrow Wilson, fell short in bringing order but it did prevent a complete take over by France and Britain.

Territorial decisions separated peoples who shared language, culture and tradition. Reparations for Germany were high, and disarmament seemed limited to Germany alone. Despite the efforts of President Wilson, the setting for another war was sliding into place soon after the Treaty of Versaille.

The Hughes Family

World War I did not affect the family directly although the docks were busy before and after the U.S. entered the fight. The boys were too young; Reg was too old. The dramatic changes affected the country and the family in other ways. Horses gave way to automobiles, skirts were raised and the radio took precedence over Sadie's songs. It was a prosperous time even with a large family and only one tragedy carried over into Sadie's later years.

The youngest child, born in Lyndhurst, had a much different experience than the others. The six children of Sarah Matilda and Reginald were equally divided by dark hair and "ginger" hair revealing the French and Scottish heritage of the family. Louise became the Chewing Gum Queen of her High School class. She was beautiful, red headed, brown-eyed and slim. And smart. The oldest boys graduated from high school and achieved high positions without the benefits of college, which came later. That was possible in the 1920's.

The media was not pervasive and there was no radio in the house until later. Somehow, Pop always knew what was happening. Maybe it was the New York carry-over or his trips around the world. By 1920, a good time was happening in the States. Music changed, telephones, ticker tape, motion pictures and automobiles were about to enter everyday life. Women began to assert their right to their own choices. Demobilization of the military guaranteed new construction and a surge of buying. The pay off of war debts to Washington led to prosperity for the many instead of the few. It was a break with the past and the coming of the "jazz Age".

The post war government was led by three consecutive Republican presidents: Harding came in 1921 during the brief post-war depression and eventually, his policies of national debt reduction, reduced taxes, reduced immigration and protection of farming led to the good times under Coolidge. Harding's proposed tax cut on the wealthy came into force under Coolidge who also blocked any government attempts to regulate private business. Government funded the needed new infrastructure: roads were critical to the new automobile industry and highways replaced some of the older routes. The U.S. and Canada added an electric grid and new power plants were built. Across the country, telephone lines were added to the tree lined roads. The prosperity bubble burst in 1929 and Hoover's attempts to get business to help the country were unsuccessful.

By 1929, Marjorie was 22 and Louise a child of 6 years. The family had weathered the war years and changes were coming. As the boys began to search for their own jobs, the openings came about in part because of the war and the changes it produced. Reg had taken risks as a young man and he encouraged his boys to be venturesome. This eventually led to a disbursement of family but for the moment, all was calm.

Gordon Lakes and Saddle River, N.J.

Although Ken and Hilton were keen hunters all of their lives, the idea of fishing might have been discouraged by the family stories of Maine. They found a way to expand life in suburban Lyndhurst by moving out to northern New Jersey, a pretty unpopulated area of lakes and woods. They recruited friends and friends of friends and on a small plot of land, a log cabin was under construction. The lakes and forests of northern Jersey are well populated now, some even serve as the hub of housing developments for commuters to New York city. Before the depression years, they were providing recreational destinations for those living near the city.

The Cabin

The cabin, built by the boys and friends of the family, still stands. The grandchildren went to visit it a few years ago and it is the most rustic bit of housing in a newly upscale neighborhood still called Gordon Lakes. New York's sprawl encompassed some of the far off vacation places of the 1930's. The cabin was definitely not a Mc Mansion but it was strong.

The family gathered there many times in the '30's, romantic attachments were made and the family made memories not forgotten.

Louise remembers renting horses from a local farmer on his day off. The farm was near the Little Lake—now a heavily populated area. Mr. Decker, the owner, allowed the young folks to visit his farm and on one special day, Old Silver and Mabel were ready to take them for a ride. George galloped off while Louise clung to Mabel who routed her under the lowest branches in the apple orchard. Hilton and Doris were properly seated in a buggy. They had hitched the horse well, too well, and when "Big Mac" pooped all over Doris the day lost some of its luster. Doris was not happy but a near-by brook was used to wash her off and the only lasting problem was the continued laughing from the boys for the rest of the day.

Long after the young folks had left for their new lives far from home, Sadie and Reg, the two old folks and their grand daughter, Jean, drove away from Lyndhurst for a new kind of lifestyle. Ken had bought a house in Saddle Brook as insurance for his own return to the States. When it was ready for occupancy, Sadie, Reg, Marjorie and Jean would live there for a time. That small gap in timing necessitated a few months of life in the cabin. Marjorie stayed with friends to continue her job in the city but the house in Lyndhurst was sold.

Sadie and Reg tooled off in their Terraplane, a car built by the Hudson Motor Car Company of Detroit, Michigan between 1932 and 1938. It was the first fully enclosed car that was affordable to the general public, a sort of Volkswagon of the day. Orville Wright bought one and so did Reg Hughes. The 8-cylinder engine gave the car easy handling and quick good acceleration, features appreciated by John Dillinger and Baby Face Nelson. It was a good car.

The Terraplane moved along the highway towards Gordon Lakes well. As they approached the lake road Jean called out, "there's Mr. Hunt!" This prompted her Grandfather to look and that caused the car to go off the road into a shallow ditch. Calling out messages was then forbidden during driving. The weekly shopping trip was equally exciting. Pappy explained that he saw three of everything and just aimed for the middle. He didn't wear glasses and no one ever challenged his license to drive.

A log cabin in summer is a dream. It was early fall. The blaze of color added a glow to the dirt road in front of the driveway. A mossy front yard sloped down to the road and across from that a steeper slope ended at the dock and the Big Lake. More like a large pond than a lake but a challenge to swim in because of the multitude of fish and turtles that competed for space. The older sons had built the cabin to accommodate summer sports. A porch went the length of one side and on entering the cabin, a huge room without doors could embrace all six grown children, wives, friends and family. Two of the sons met and married girls from Gordon Lakes. Marjorie always went back with a sense of loss—this was where she and Bill had courted.

There were built in beds along every wall. In the daytime they were couches. A big table, brought up from the Lyndhurst house, filled the center of the lower part of the room. A cast iron stove faced the back porch. The kitchen was small, the one bedroom was smaller, and the only bath was not a bath but an inside toilet and sink. It was made to provide a quick facility for the hunters, not comfort for women and children.

These were difficult times for Sadie and Reg. The cabin was isolated and lacked some basic amenities they had grown used to having. There was running water and an inside john but no shower or tub. The stove provided heat if well fed, the grocery store was far away in Butler with only a small local store about 2 miles up the road.

At the cabin, six year old Jean made herself at home. The bedroom was hers as she was sent to bed early. Each weekday morning she was bussed to a one-room schoolhouse, walking about a mile to the bus stop each morning. The walk went past the closed summer houses of the development and at six, it was a pleasure to be alone. At night she read with a flashlight under the covers. Dammy would call, "Jean, are you still awake?" She would answer, "no". But W.W. Jacobs was her companion as he had been her grandfather's. The stories from the ships at sea were like those her Grandfather told her and if she missed some of the nuances of character it was a small loss. The pictures of barrel bellied sailors gave an incredible impression of maritime workers.

Fall quickly fell into winter. The only house still lit was the cabin. The school bus still ran, picking up children from further down the road for the trip into Butler. The walk became a sort of trot as the winds of winter practiced on the lake road. This time was about to end.

By late November the house bought by Uncle Ken was ready and the "cabin dwellers" moved back to civilization. Jean was placed in second grade as a reader. Teachers were astounded that a child could enter their school as an expert reader after attending a one-room schoolhouse in the outback. There was a bus for the youngest children that stopped at the front door and the early morning walks were no longer necessary. The Franklin Avenue School became the daily destination.

The house on Sterling Place had room for cats. Snookie took up residence and she prospered. There was a sun porch the length of the house, cheerful even in winter. Another fireplace to look into, another dining room and a small but serviceable kitchen that produced kippers, cod fish cakes and stewed tomatoes regularly. Upstairs had a large bedroom and one slightly smaller. At night the radio brought in Amos and Andy. And the news. Pap was a dedicated follower of the news, a devoted fan of Franklin Delano Roosevelt and no one disputed his choice.

In the last year of school in Saddle River, the grandparents became in need of more help. Marjorie helped her younger sister and husband to buy a house in Hackettstown where they could add a small apartment for the old folks. So Dammy and Pappy moved, the Saddle Brook house sold quickly. Marjorie again looked for a home. The oldest brother finally found them a place with his wife's parents in East Paterson.

By the early '50's, Reg and Sarah moved to Hackettstown with Doris and her husband Claude. They all lived in a second floor apartment while a house with attached apartment was built on Center Street. Marjorie received a steady stream of letters during this time and the big news was the move—Sadie would be able to walk through the new house without the aid of the Rescue Squad and the change to a quiet back street was enthusiastically welcomed.

Pop still kept the "old jalopy" or the Blue Hornet as he had named the Terraplane. He praised its engine but was concerned about the state of its body. This car lasted well and by 1952 Reg felt it was still worth about $150.

There was a last bit of traveling for Reginald and a new adventure for Sadie in those last years. They traveled together by boat to Diablo Heights, Canal Zone, Panama, to visit Hilton, his wife Clare and daughter Nancy. Hilton arranged a dinner at the Atlas Club with champagne and much applause. Reg spoke over the airwaves—his early fascination with radio fulfilled—as he answered questions about past experiences at sea. He also noted that Sadie had kept all the letters he wrote her while his was away over the years. Sadie wrote that she felt faint but it was all lovely. Sadie's letter home to Marjorie on September 15, 1948 is as follows:

"My dear Marjorie and Jean, I have just read your Dad's letter over and he has forgotten to tell you about his birthday party. Claire had a very large cake and she and Hilton got fun out of the number of candles -75- that were put on it and Dad had to go to the bathroom and low and behold it was about burning the cake up before he got back! I think he was crying in there. Then at eleven o'clock they sang to him—'Mr. Reginald Hughes is 75 today' and this was over the radio. Kenneth and Bea with the children were here and we had a very pleasant time but I missed you and Jeanie also Doris and family, George and Pat and little Joan. In fact, all of you—I love you all so much. I am glad Pop writes—he is better at it than I in letting you know the news but I shall write you when you say you have kissed little (?). So with lots of love to you both, Mom p.s. We are at Hilton's and get the mail much quicker as the P.O. is near-by. It is raining and so cold I think it will snow.

Sarah Matilda Emery Hughes

Reginald died on February 17, 1953 at his home in Hackettstown. His 79 years were well spent. Sarah Emery Hughes died at age 74 on March 15, 1955. She lived to hold her first great-grandson, Steve, although she was in a nursing home. At the time of their deaths, their children followed the pattern of the times. Kenneth lived in Honduras, Central America, Hilton was still in Panama working in the Canal Zone, but George, Marjorie and Louise were close at hand. The couple spent their last five years living in an apartment attached to the home of their daughter, Doris, and her husband, Claude Kraft, in Hackettstown, New Jersey. Sarah and Reginald are buried in Cresthaven Memorial Park, Clifton, New Jersey, far from their Nova Scotia and Maine beginnings.

Sarah was survived by her six children: Marjorie of Saddle River, New Jersey; Kenneth of Honduras, C.A.; Hilton of Balboa, Canal Zone; Doris of Hackettstown; George of Bloomfield, New Jersey and Louise of West Palm Beach, Florida.

A steady stream of letters came from her last home in Hackettstown to her children. Any problems were shared amongst the sons and daughters who did their best to keep the old folks aware of only the good news. Sadie Emery Hughes saved all the letters written by her husband while he was at sea. Those seem gone. Reg and Sadie, always a page from each, wrote their children regularly. Those letters on fragile paper are still in the families' hands. Email is wonderful but the feel of those letters is a more tangible link to the past.

Throughout their lives, Sadie and Reg were close to water. They lived in many places, more like their great-grandparents than their parents. While both sides of the family had connections to the sea, Reg was the family member who traveled furthest and longest over his long career. His granddaughter married a ship's Captain she met while living with her parents, Ken and Bea, in Honduras. Living far from water is a difficult choice for any of the family and it provided for them very well.

The Hughes family was tightly linked to the Cunard line for most of the 19th and 20th centuries. Reginald Hughes was born in Annapolis Royale and a proud employee of Cunard for most of his working life. The Cunard Line, now linked to Carnival cruises, still exists. It is the last surviving operator of scheduled ocean liner service. The Queen Victoria has a 1,980 berth and the Queen Elizabeth, whose maiden voyage was in October 2010, holds 2,068. The 1929 crises in shipping led the British government to broker a deal between the International Mercantile Marine Company, backed by J. Pierpoint Morgan, and Cunard. With Cunard and the White Star Line merged in 1934, the line had new life. In 1947 the Cunard Company bought out White Star's share and the name Cunard returned to shipping in 1950. The old Cunard Line Building still stands on lower Broadway near the huge sculpture by Modica titled "Charging Bull" and placed in Bowling Green Park, seemingly to honor Wall Street.

XII

Sarah's Daughters

Marjorie

Descendent of sea captains, Tories, patriots, farmers and schoolteachers, Marjorie was the oldest of the six children and the enforcer of discipline for her siblings. Her brothers described her stern use of a stick and the complete lack of a carrot when she was in charge. She never lost her feeling of responsibility for the welfare of the extended family, always in touch and ready to help.

In Lyndhurst, the kitchen was the main gathering place and full of activity. The eight chairs that served the table had festoons of heavy wire holding them together. Intricate knots kept the legs from parting but occasionally one would give way and dump its occupant. Marjorie grew up with the sound of singing. Unfortunately, and despite the Welsh connection, all of it was extremely off key. Sadie sang The Trail of the Lonesome Pine often, Reg muttered something unrecognizable and claimed the tunes were sea chanties. Until Louise brought modern music into the house, the sound was joyous but not pleasing. In contrast, Sadie knew many poems by heart—favorites by Shakespeare and Oliver Wendell Holmes were better than her lullabies. She even wrote some of her own. It was a noisy house and the player piano filled in when the quiet was overwhelming.

Reg was listed in an early census as Anglican—a possible clue of the families early Loyalist sentiments. In later years, even when raising his own family, religion was not part of their lives. Sadie often told her granddaughter that she was a Christian Scientist and her meaning was unclear enough to be accepted as the path to be followed by her grand daughter.

Marjorie finished 8th grade in 1921. She did well and continued at Kearny High School with a program of typing, commercial arithmetic, bookkeeping and spelling. This was considered a suitable place to end public school so in place of high school, she attended the Egan School of Business in Hackensack for one year. Both entering and leaving this school were bittersweet events. She loved school and felt that she had become a woman of the world much too soon. After business school, her shorthand and typing expertise helped her to move into her first job. Marjorie was 15 and jobs were plentiful even with the returning military in competition. Her father came home one day and announced, "you have a job and it starts tomorrow." It was in Hoboken at American Smelting and Refining, a firm where the family had a friend. Pop took her to the train and she became an employee of a plumbing company. The money she earned was helpful at home and there was no thought of independent living. The boys were growing up but stayed in school. They had private thoughts of leaving home and learned not to share them.

At home, Marjorie was accepted as part of the family financial base. Very little of her time was spent on frivolous pastimes—there was a new baby at home and her help was needed. And she was far too young to go out on her own except with a few friends on the block. Pop kept the family up to date on world affairs. He now had a radio. The exploits of Lindbergh were discussed along with diaper rash and the heavy cost of commuting.

Marjorie saw her brothers graduate from high school. When the opportunity came, Hilton left for work on the Panama Canal and then, Ken, the oldest brother, followed. Their title was Engineer, one ran the roundhouse and the other managed the locks. When war came, their country expected them to stay at the canal and they did. Both had married, children were born in the Canal Zone and lived in modest homes with a number of nannies, maids, yard workers and helpers. Sadie never accepted their leaving and still complained that it was these two who broke up the family.

Marjorie's best friend was Ruth, who also commuted to work. Ruth had a large family and when she married, it came with her. Two tantes, Marika and Mimi moved in with the young couple. And through this family, Marjorie met a young man who was a cousin. Bill was a Rutgers graduate, and to Marjorie, he was almost godlike. He had studied Latin and Greek. His acceptance at Rutgers was through an understanding that he intended to enter the clergy. Farthest thought from his mind. He was small but played football with Rutgers. A willingness to get injured in any reckless endeavor led him to a trip west on his own and numerous hair-raising accidents on a motorcycle. Through it all, he stayed close to his mother and eventually came home to get his first job, not in a church, but on a newspaper.

It was 1928. In Europe factories increased production and Germany was rising once again. The new family could be considered middle class—a college educated father embarked on a life-long career devoted to hunting and fishing. His newspaper columns were well received and his time on the road expanded. The house was new. It had two bedrooms, a bath, and the customary kitchen, dining room and living room. The house had a mother, father and soon after, a baby girl. For many reasons, the marriage did not last. The brick house was put on the market and Marjorie became the major breadwinner. Marjorie and child moved back to the Lyndhurst house. It was closer to her job and the grandparents agreed to watch the youngster who was now in school. And so late in life, Sadie and Reg undertook the raising of another child just 10 years younger than their last.

The master bedroom had a huge closet and a dressing room/bath. It was perfect for babies starting out but by the time Jean lived there it's main feature was the closet where her aunt would lock the door and say, "see you" while humming "A tisket a tasket" on her way down to the kitchen. Her aunt was a scant 10 years older and more like a sister. Neighbors had gossiped that Louise was really Marjorie's child when she was born. She was the darling of her parents, beautiful, intelligent and ready to make her mark. Louise left to marry at a very young age, to begin life away from home.

Things changed with the family decision to make life easier for the old folks, Reginald and Sadie. Two of their three sons were at work on the Panama Canal. Another was a banker in Cuba. It was decided that the hunting cabin the boys built at Gordon Lakes could be an interim home for the grandparents and Marjorie, after the Lyndhurst home sold and before another house was ready for occupancy in Saddle River. The older brother now had children of his own and wanted a foothold back in the states. Marjorie had a good job but would rent a room locally, sending Jean with her grandparents.

Marjorie was moving up from clerk to secretary to assistant to the Company President during this time. Her job was important to her but she always had the support of family and friends and years later she noted this as the biggest blessing of her life.

When she was almost 90 years of age, Marjorie patiently answered questions in a Great Grandmother's book brought to Connecticut by grandson Charles' wife, Teresa. Marjorie worked until she was 72 and then lived in Connecticut—a place she always saw as a poor substitute for New York City. Looking back, her pride was in her job and the recognition she received for her work. She was amazed to note that in her lifetime radio, telephones, television, automobiles, computers, space ships and antibiotics all appeared—as if by magic. She was most awed by the discovery of a cure and preventative for polio as the memories of the epidemics of the past were still real. But her favorite invention of the time was carry-out and she was sure it would have made life better than any other new invention.

Doris

The middle child and middle daughter had all the traits of her ancestors. She loved her family and took care of them all when needed. She was calm, patient, hard-working and well loved. Doris had a strong marriage. Anything that Claude said was received as gospel, anything he did was heroic, and anything he wanted was supplied if possible.

And he deserved all the accolades. He was a devoted husband and father, adapting to the strange decisions of his off-spring who chose college rather than inheriting a business and who left home for far-away places when work beckoned.

Doris and Claude provided a home for Sadie and Reg in their last years. It was not an easy assignment although the others tried to be supportive.

Her daughter, Marilyn, wrote this short biography. Doris was born on November 4, 1914 in Yonkers, N.Y., the fourth child of Sarah and Reginald. She was often the butt of pranks played by her older brothers but as a result, she developed her own sense of humor that carried her through many crises later in life.

She loved visits to the farm owned by her mother's brother Everett. Old Silver, his horse, was not a favorite but she forgave his lapses. Her high school career followed Marjorie's and she later worked as a bookkeeper at J.C.

Penney in N.Y.C. And like her sister, she lived at home and gave her salary to her parents with a bit left for fares and lunch.

She was married to Claude Kraft in 1939. At first, they lived in Pleasantville, N.J. where he worked for an Ice Cream shop. When their first son, Robert, was born they moved back to Lyndhurst. Marilyn was also born in Lyndhurst. Soon after, Claude and his brother bought a building in Hackettstown, N.J. to open a paint store. Sadie and Reg moved in with them in later years, first on Mill Street and then in a new house on Center Street. All four spent the remainder of their lives in that house.

A third child, Edward, was born in 1949. Doris raised her three children and cared for her parents with grace and without complaint. She was active at church, a Girl Scout leader and an officer in the Hackettstown Rescue Squad Auxiliary when Claude served as a dedicated charter member of the group.

Marilyn wrote a special tribute as follows: "One of her greatest attributes was her unconditional love. She loved from her own character, integrity, and capacity. Her love did not depend on your actions or who you were or what you did. Loving her siblings and friends in this way made her a happier person and loving her children this way taught them what true love really is. She had a deep, quiet faith. Prayer was important to her and she used it to handle any problems or concerns even when suffering Altzheimer's disease."

Claude died in 1995 and Doris went to live in Houston, TX near her daughter. Doris went to be "with her Lord and Savior January 25, 1998."

Louise

Louise was the beneficiary of the traveler's dreams. She married young, later married again and then set off on her own adventures after the death of her husband. Both husbands were in service and over the years Louise attended numerous Air Force, Army and Navy schools, taking coursework in Defense Contract Management and Fiscal and Contract Law. Her B.A. degree was completed through the University of Maryland while she was stationed overseas. During Louise's marriage to Capt. Maurice J. Plank of the USAF, she used her time well. Capt. Plank flew a bomber during WWII at the same time her brother, George Hughes flew a P-47 Thunderbolt escort. Captain Plank also fought in the Korean War and retired in 1961. He died in 1963.

At that time, Louise resumed her federal civil service career and was employed at Homestead Air Force Base as a secretary and later, a buyer for the Air Force. During her time at Homestead, The Bay of Pigs debacle turned the base into an armed camp for many months. In 1974, Louise transferred to the US Army Corps of Engineers, Far East District, and received a promotion to the position of Contract Specialist, posted in Seoul, Korea. The Corps built large installations and bridges throughout South Korea on a quid pro-quo basis. Another undertaking was the locating of tunnels being excavated by the North to accommodate the transit of large armored vehicles capable of transporting soldiers for attacks on South Korea.

She made strong attempts at learning the language but found it better to use pidgin English to be understood.

Basically, there was no literal translation as many learning a second language find out and the idiomatic and grammatic structure of Korean was more than difficult. The Korean language had a mix left by many who made a path through the country in the past—a bit of Mongol, Chinese, Japanese and even Persian composed the vocabulary.

A special concern she wrote home about were the mixed children—part American, part Korean who were abandoned by their parents. They were not allowed to attend school and the lowest jobs were held by these orphans of the war as they grew to adulthood.

She also saw the smog drift in more and more with time. Some wore surgical masks, especially in winter when charcoal was used for heating. Other things came up over time, for example, the beauty of some Korean products was known but not used by Koreans—all the best was exported.

The liberated Louise did her best to hide her objections to the role of women but she did shake a fist at several maniacal male drivers and to make a point, she nominated a female for employee of the year. The woman won. Louise supervised many men as her job moved up to Acting Chief of Procurement and Supply. She consciously practiced diplomacy on a daily basis.

Living in the Namsan Apartment complex brought problems for many Americans housed there. The bills were exorbitant but Korean Electric was owned by the Government and untouchable for renters' complaints. Louise noted in a letter home that she had her horoscope fully developed and it told her she was destined to "have trouble with authority figures". She wished then that mom had given birth when her planets were better aligned.

A transfer was arranged in 1981. Louise was promoted to Contracting Officer in the 8th Army Contracting Agency. Her job was to handle the smaller construction and service contracts for all military installations in South Korea. This was a heavy responsibility at all times but especially so when the Army and Air Force conducted combined war maneuvers. Today, Louise comments that the efforts of the combined US forces have kept the North Koreans at bay for the last 50 plus years.

Another transfer sent Louise to the US Army Corps of Engineers, Middle East District, in the desert near the town of Hafar-al-Batin. The Corps constructed a military city on that site which was practical and luxurious. Only the best materials were used in construction and it was featured on US television's 60 Minutes. Prince Sultan escorted Harry Reasoner through many of the underground installations and appeared on camera with Reasoner, a rare event. The site was near the borders of Kuwait and Iraq. During Desert Storm, Iraqi soldiers had to be driven back from the border, however, they managed to land some SCUD missiles on or near KKMC.

Louise went to Saudi Arabia as an employee of the Army Corps of Engineers. She described King Khalid Military city in Al Balin as an isolated outpost in the middle of the desert. The site was apparently chosen because underground water supplies were available. The U.S. Army Engineer Division/Middle East Corps of Engineers were in Saudi in 1984 to plan and implement construction for the Kingdom of Saudi Arabia's Ministry of

Defense and Aviation. Strict rules of behavior dominated the atmosphere and most were carefully obeyed.

In July 1985, she returned to the US and worked for the next three years with the Defense Contracts Administration Agency located in the Martin-Marietta plant in Orlando, Florida. She retired in March 1988 and received a Distinguished Career Award from the Defense Logistics Agency for 29 years of service. During those 29 years, Louise travelled to Hawaii, the Far East, Middle East and Europe.

The children of the last Sarah carried the characteristics of their predecessors. The call of new places affected them all, except perhaps Doris, the family oriented daughter who most copied her mother, maternal grandmother and great-grandmother.

The daughters reflected the changes of the times. Their choices were not always honored but they adapted to circumstances unthought of in the 19th century. While they did not labor physically to the extent of Sarah Morang and Sarah MacDonald, they most certainly did battle for themselves and their family in the marketplace, the home and the society.

While her education effectively ended in grade 8, Marjorie moved up the career ladder in New York City. Doris married and raised her own family of two boys and a girl while taking over the responsibilities of the two old folks in the early 1950's. And Louise became the true adventurer, seeing the most exotic places, working and living in them as well.

Marjorie, Louise, Jean, Doris

The Hughes Family in the New Century

Marjorie commuted to her job in NYC in one capacity or another until she was 72 years of age. She was well respected and moved up the ladder to become executive secretary to one and then another engineer. Her contacts with employees coming into central office from South America, Idaho and Europe were a source of interest and learning. She wanted to travel and she eventually did see most of the places she had heard and read about. A special visit to Shakespeare's home in England linked her with her mother's love of theater. And before her brothers came back to the states, she saw the Canal, stood in the control tower and operated the locks with some help.

Kenneth and Hilton had stayed on in the Canal Zone, working for the U.S. government through the war years and after. Claire wrote a letter from the Canal Zone in October 1950, they were anxious to come home by Christmas. Hilton wrote that the prices in the Canal Zone were rising fast, and, for the first time an income tax had been levied, retroactive to January 1, 1950. The Governor had informed them that he had to make up a $4 million deficit and he chose an income tax as the best way to do it. Another son was now looking for a job at home.

Hilton did return Stateside and bought a place on Rangely Lake in Maine. It was full circle for at least one member of the family. His second home was in Florida, more like the climate he enjoyed in Panama. Kenneth stayed on in Central America and raised his family in Honduras as an engineer for United Fruit.

Doris was the rock of the family. Even tempered and family oriented, she married and seemed to provide shelter for almost every family member over time, ending with the job of caretaker for Sadie and Reg while raising her own three children.

George, the youngest son, was in the US Naval Reserve from 1934-1938, cruising on two Destroyers and two Battleships. He was in the Essex Troop of the N.J. National Guard, 102nd Calvary in 1938. George joined the U.S. Airforce in 1942 and trained in Oklahoma and Texas as a fighter pilot. He was assigned to the 295th fighter group as a P-47 pilot. George was stationed in Winchester, England and flew 4 missions on D-Day in the first Air Squadron to move into France. Of the 25 pilots in his squad, 18 were killed in action.

He served in the Army Air Corps during the war— the only family member to be on active duty, flying an escort fighter plane over Germany until stricken with pneumonia. He remembered his 72 hour "shifts" on these flights as one of the problems of duty.

By 1948, he was living in Havana, Cuba on foreign duty with the Chase Manhattan Bank. He, wife Pat who had also served in the war as a Radio Operator, and their baby Joan, were eager to return to the States, with or without a job. He wrote Marjorie and felt badly that the Lyndhurst house was gone.

Louise celebrates her 91st birthday in June 2013. Her home in Ocala, Florida is airy and spacious. She cultivated local contacts to help with heavy cleaning and gardening but she is independent and can be contacted by email. Louise remains connected to the times and has definite opinions On Politics, entertainers, family, and travel. She drives a new Buick and it talks to her, a far cry from the Terraplane.

Sarah's Grandchildren

The days of large families seem to be over. It is no longer practical to raise 12 children to assure help on the farm. It is not practical to have a small farm. The impossibility of educating 10 or more children to compete in the modern world would give most parents pause and so Sarah and Reg left 12 grandchildren to carry on the family story. Only 4 are males and only two carry the family name.

Ken Hughes, son of Kenneth, lives in Maine. Bob Hughes, son of Hilton, lives in Florida. This seems as far apart as geography and culture can place the two who carry the Hughes name. The granddaughters are equally separated.

Jean, daughter of Marjorie, is in Connecticut, Beatrice and Carol, daughters of Kenneth, are in Maine but Beverly is a long time resident of Lake George in upper New York state. Marilyn, Doris' daughter makes her home in Crockett, Texas and George's daughter is in Franklin, New Jersey. Doris' sons, Bob and Ed are also far apart: Bob in Cincinnati, Ohio and Ed in New Jersey. Joan Alexis is the connector of the kin. She is steeped in the far past, the middle past, and the present through Ancestry.com, emails and letters. We all owe her a debt of gratitude for explaining how we arrived at our current locations!

As Sadie feared, the family has no true home but technology keeps them connected.

The grandchildren followed many paths but none have been directly involved in wars. The timing placed their parents in World War II but the Korean and Vietnam Wars did not happen when they were eligible for service. All have become part of the new fabric of the country in very different ways.

The overlapping of events made the earlier families closer. Wars and their effects were shared and the politics that built the background of those wars deeply affected the lives of the three Sarahs. Although the French and Indian or began in 1754 and ended with the Treaty of

Paris in 1763, it was surely a determinant in the move of Sarah Morang's parents.

This war had its roots in Europe as Great Britain and France struggled for the control of North America. French colonists, Anglo–American colonists, and the Iroquois Confederacy all were in the mix on the frontiers of claimed land. While fighting escalated on the frontiers on North American field of contest, Britain and France continued their battles over India, the Caribbean Islands, Spanish Cuba and the Phillipines where commerce was the prize.

Britain emerged victorious but the expense of the war led to new taxes on the American colonies. This and other errors of Imperial authority hastened the coming of the war for Independence and the birth of a new nation in North America.

The cultural backgrounds of the three Sarahs provided difficult choices exacerbated by conflicts with "mother countries" involved in spreading their reach. From Maine to New York, all made the choice to become part of the United States.

XIII

The Economy as History: Depressions, Recessions and Taxes

I n 1776, the balance of economic power was shifting to the American colonies and the standard of living for the free white American population was bolstered by the abundance of food and land. The new Constitution assured the regulation of commerce and money through the Congress and open borders promoted the internal free flow of goods.

A tax on whiskey was enacted in 1791 to help pay down the national debt, a result of the Revolutionary War. Leading into the new century, regional economies featured shipyards in New England, crops in middle America, and the plantation economy of the south. Gordon writes that one man, Samuel Slater, a textile manufacturer relocating from England, brought the British textile industry to America. Eli Whitney's cotton gin raised the South to elevated status with cotton and slavery as its foundation. The discovery of gold in 1848 called many west to California and the country was expanding to its current frontiers. As Sarah Morang grew and raised her family in Maine, the frontier opened through waterways plied by steamboats, and railroads that linked east and west and triumphantly finished with the Transcontinental Railroad in 1869.

Taxes became reality with the first federal income tax and a precursor of the IRS established in 1861. During the years of the Civil War, the national debt grew 80 times its pre-Civil War size.

Financial crises abound in the years spanning the lives of the three Sarahs, despite the policies and principles of different administrations. Sarah Morang, born in1806, was introduced to financial hard times when the depression of 1807-1814 came as a result of President Thomas Jefferson's trade embargo. His goal was to keep the young nation from involvement in the wars of Europe, specifically the fight for supremacy waged by Britain and France. His concerns were exacerbated by the British view that American sailors were British citizens who could be removed from their United States vessels and taken into the service of British ships. The trade embargo set in place severely affected the fledgling industries in the States, cut imports into the United States but shifted home production for the benefit of the domestic market. If the recession had not affected the ability of citizens to purchase goods, the results may have been better. Jefferson's high hopes were dashed and the War of 1812 finally led to the end of the trade embargo and the recovery of the economy.

By 1836, when Congress passed the Distribution Act, treasury surpluses moved to State banks. Banks were required to pay State government in specie (gold and silver). President Andrew Jackson's Specie Circular imposed a regulation that required specie only in payment for government land. This effectively reduced money in circulation and depreciated the value of banknotes. And so, deflation followed along with the failure of many budding enterprises, including farming, as those expecting to make money on their crops were faced with lower prices.

This was a factor in the settlements of former farmers from Missouri to the lands held by Mexico. The battle of the Alamo was fought by many who had traveled west to settle and start again.

Railroads spread across the new nation at a rapid rate, aided by government assistance with land acquisition. One impediment was the Gold Standard as the holdings in gold could not keep pace with the growth of the economy. The burgeoning interest in rail maintained demand for iron and steel and so all three thriving industries were affected. Companies like the railroad investment firm of Jay Cooke and Co. moved into bankruptcy.

From 1893 to 1898, a severe economic depression is documented, starting in 1893 with the financial failure of the Philadelphia and Reading Railroad and shortly after, the failure of the National Cordage Company. In that same year, the Erie Railroad, The Union Pacific and the Atchison, Topeka and Santa Fe all folded. In this financial panic, 500 banks and 16,000 businesses felt the pangs of bankruptcy. This panic, as for many, was caused largely by unregulated development and financial speculation.

The huge number of bank failures during the panic of 1907 under Theodore Roosevelt finally moved the Wilson administration to action. By 1913, Congress passed the Federal Reserve Act. Opposition by private banks did not prevail. Twelve federal districts were formed, each with its own Federal Reserve Bank. The original structure has been changed many times but there continue to be banks for bankers and member banks.

Advances in technology mark the early 20th century. When the US entered World War I, industrial efforts and raw materials were switched from consumer products to wartime production. The method of financing this war and the military was the focus addressed by the 1917 War Revenue Act to raise taxes and the public purchase of war bonds. The new Federal Reserve was well on the way to becoming the financial center of the world.

In the 21st century, the seven members of the Board of Governors are appointed by the President and confirmed by the Senate to a 14-year term of office. A Chair and Vice-Chair serve a four-year term. The primary function of the Board is the formulation of monetary policy. Reserve requirements include the discount rate, margin requirements and open market operations. These are the functions regulated and supervised by the Federal Reserve System. The Board meets several times weekly and regularly confers with officials of other government agencies, banking industry group representatives, members of Congress, academicians and officials of the central banks of other countries.

Historians and economists agree that the definitive events of the 20th century are the Great Depression and World War II. Franklin Roosevelt's New Deal was a stimulus package that sponsored public works projects, initiated a Federal Deposit Insurance Corporation (FDIC) and underwrote mortgages through Fannie Mae. The role of Federal Government expanded and a close relationship between the private sector and the government developed to rebuild the country.

The efforts of both government and private business were necessary for the mobilization of all resources for the war effort. The GNP, Gross National Product, increased over 50% between 1941 and 1945 and unemployment was measured at 1.2%. After the war, the country continued to grow, aided by the completion of the Interstate Highway system, the largest public works project in the history of the world according to Gordon.

Roots and New Shoots Considered

Job Growth and the Economy

Economists predict a steady growth in the economy in the second half of 2013 with new jobs in the offing. The deficit is still a mantra for pessimists' predicting a melt-down. The stimulus either saved or doomed the recovery from the recession of 2007, depending on your political point of view. The cuts to social programs are certainly on the table in 2013 and the attitude is one somewhat related to Social Darwinism on the one side and a civilized response to assistance of the poor, elderly and disabled on the other. A large difference of opinion is clear on taxation: should the top 1% pay less than the rest of taxpayers? Democrats argue for increased tax revenue combined with spending cuts. Republicans oppose any tax increases on the wealthy or on corporations.

Recorded business cycles with their peaks and troughs are listed by the National Bureau of Economic Research (NBEC) beginning in 1854. From that year to 2009, there were 33 cycles with an average duration of 11.1 months and approximately 69.5 months between each cycle. The severity of the contraction of December, 2007 had begun to ameliorate by June 2009.

The National Bureau of Economic Research, Inc., located in Cambridge, Massachusetts, published turning points after 1979. The specific definition of a recession is as follows: "a significant decline in economic activity spread across the economy, lasting more than a few months, normally visible in the real GDP, real income, employment, industrial production, and wholesale-retail sales." It is a definition worth considering but the occurrence of a recession is not a new phenomenon. The greatest contraction determined by the NBEC was of 43 months from peak to trough. The dates are from the peak in August 1929 to the trough in March 1933.

What is of interest is the effect of cyclical contractions on democratic societies. As the global economy replaced small agrarian nations, the impact of financial stress became the cause of many political changes, some leading to wars.

An article by Rana Foroohar in Time magazine wrote about the economy of 2012. She noted that it is not possible to have a sustainable recovery in an "economy that's 70% fueled by consumer spending when 90% of the income gains since the recovery began have accrued to 1% of the population." People in the top 1% don't need stuff, they already have it.

Foroohar explains that the International Monetary Fund's research arm shows that countries with the largest wealth gaps tend to have shorter periods of high growth and more volatility. This happens most specifically when inequality is hidden by the expansion of consumer credit. Many economists believe reducing inequality is a key factor in improving economic growth. Do markets begin at home, or does the sophisticated world interact on the basis of the best supplier?

Globalization: One World

Industrialization changed the trajectory of history in the 19th century and by adding technology, globalization is complete. If seeking a date to note the time when nation states became of less importance than the whole of the planet, there is an interesting search ahead.

World War II changed the power base of nations and America became the source for rebuilding parts of Europe left in ruins. The US was considered the richest nation in the world in the early '50's and the emphasis on building infrastructure at home helped establish the industrial sector of the economy. President Dwight D. Eisenhower, who served as General of the ETO in WWII, greatly expanded the highway system but warned of the coming dominance of the "military–industrial" complex as he left office.

The European Common Market and the Euro have united traditional enemies through a common currency but diverse economic policies are also in place. Portugal, Italy, Greece, and Spain wobble on the edge of financial ruin while requesting aid from the most financially stable countries, including Germany. The days of colonial expansion seem over and the pain of national contraction is evident.

While land occupation is ending, the piracy of ideas is well underway. Some technological drift to China can be laid at the door of out-sourcing; some is more innovative. Combined with the power of the state in China and North Korea, the lot of the laborer progresses with painful difficulty. Japan suffered a severe economic set-back almost 10 years past, it has not yet reached former levels. The destruction of a major nuclear power complex by tsunami, only two years ago has further delayed its recovery.

India's educational system was a legacy from the British Raj. The emphasis on education did not extend to all citizens but the structure was in place. India's tech expertise is shown in many journals dedicated to the use of technology and the practice of out-sourcing by the western hemisphere helped India develop the most expeditious call-centers on the globe, used by many countries to maintain contacts and to increase sales. Other countries in the region do not do as well but they are providing the labor for major players in the garment trade worldwide.

Latin America grows well. Brazil and Argentina are sound and Venezuela has become a powerhouse due to their wealth of oil. Indeed, the newest Pope, Francis, is from Argentina, recognition of the growing Catholic Church in South America.

Slave trade is no longer a threat in Africa, at least from western nations. The internal conflicts have brought death and disease to too many people from Mali, Somalia and others in that region. In northern Africa, the Arab Spring unleashed the power of the common man but often without leadership, unifying principles, or a roadmap to achieving goals acceptable to all.

Civil Rights are at issue globally. One's definition of a Right is tempered by culture, history, status, financial base, and even language. The diamond miner in South Africa has different aspirations from Muslims in Paris or garment workers in Bangladesh. Who will champion the underdogs in the new century?

One World Economy

There have been over 30 cycles of expansion and recession in the US Economy since 1854 according to the National Bureau of Economic Research. When markets are booming, speculation and overvaluation create a bull market. Modica's "Charging Bull" on Wall Street is there to stay.

In present times, the bull market came to an end when interest rates rose and investments in technology slowed. In 2007 the subprime mortgage bubble burst. Unregulated lending practices are blamed in part, most specifically adjustable-rate mortgages and resultant defaults. Asset-backed securities bundled with subprime mortgages collapsed in value, and as Ferguson states, the bundled loans sent shocks felt around the world. The Federal Reserve system did prevent an explosion of small bank failures but many lost their savings in other ways.

While austerity (some imposed not chosen by the recipients of aide) has been an answer in some countries, for example Greece; the US opted for stimulus. The importance of the responses lies more in the global nature of bust now than it did in former years.

World War II changed the economy of the world. Agriculture in the USA became a more mechanized process and the industry of the country helped to rebuild parts of Europe left in ruins. The fast growth of post-war America was hastened by the consumer needs of returning military and the resultant baby-boom. The children born then are the retiring "boomers" of the 21st century, stretching the resources hard hit by the depression beginning in 2007.

The nation was considered the richest in the world in the early '50's and the growth of its infrastructure helped to establish the industrial sector of the economy. With the collapse of the Soviet Union, dominance belonged to the USA. President Dwight D. Eisenhower who served as General of the Army in WWII greatly expanded the highway system but warned of the "military-industrial" complex on leaving office.

XIV

Progress

Education: The Equalizer

Despite the anguish of the Civil War, President Lincoln signed the Morrill Act to grant land to the states to ensure the establishment of public colleges. Named the "land grant college act" its true effect was to open higher education to more Americans. While classical college courses still were in existence in the oldest institutions, the new colleges would add to their base and promote specialized training in agriculture, engineering, manufacturing and applied fields of learning. The students leaving these colleges were the engine for rebuilding the country after the Civil War.

Like Lincoln's land grant colleges, the GI Bill signed by President Roosevelt promoted the growth of an educated middle class composed of returning veterans of WWII. This action would increase the productivity and creativity of the American economy. It is estimated that one-half of the 16 million veterans who served took advantage of this opportunity to continue their education.

President Harry Truman brought more change through the establishment of a Commission on Higher Education and the doubling of college attendance in America. President Lyndon Johnson created the first federal student aid program and in 1972, President Richard Nixon expanded the program with a system of Pell grants aimed at lower income students.

Subsequent Presidents have tried to reform public education through accountability, waivers, charter schools and early childhood programs. Sputnik roused educators to consider how far other countries were out pacing the US in mathematics education. Comparisons with others now point to a need for new efforts. The advent of Science, Technology, Engineering, Math (STEM) emphasis in the early 21st century has caught the attention of educators and promoted new goals for teacher training, content proficiency testing for teacher candidates and ongoing professional development. No Child Left Behind (NCLB), a legacy from President Bush, is now showing many children left behind as schools fail to meet the goals set more than five years ago.

While we have traveled far from McGuffey's readers, literacy in high level math, science and technology courses have set new standards for public schools. Rather than looking at current teachers, an in-depth study of Institutions of Higher Education producing the new teachers is in order. Public education is the backbone of America. It deserves the respect accorded those private schools available to few and the resources to match them.

Education expanded its scope and the number of young people served over the years of the three women's lives. While all three received an education of the times, by the 21st century it is notable that fewer women than men drop out of high school, more women attend college and graduate and more are attending medical school. The daughter of Sarah Matilda Hughes became a supervisor of men during her employment with the Department of Defense in Korea, and this just little more than 60 years after women received the right to vote. The education of citizens was heightened by wars throughout these times and the elevation of women to the top tiers of business followed.

Yet education is another problem unsolved. Accountability for instruction has been the buzz for many years. A rise in teacher salaries did not seem to help. Teach for America recruits high achieving college graduates into teaching through alternative routes, a way of saying that the recruits have high content knowledge but no specific training in methodology or behavior management. It can work for a basic problem has always been teachers with inadequate knowledge of the subjects they teach. The recession has slowed the growth of magnet schools, charter schools are seen as a great advance although they have not proven to be the answer everywhere.

The ideological base of the United States followed world trends, yet it was always unique to the new nation. Philosophically, the impact of Puritans, Calvinists, Freethinkers and Social Darwinists is still very much in evidence. Our country is composed of many cultures—one out of many is a goal that lies heavy on every generation. A country without dispute and differences would not be what we expect in the U.S. despite the efforts for consensus expended by many good people.

The Environment

From the mid-19th century until the dawn of the 20th, the Congress of the United States passed only three measures related to natural resources. The rapid industrialization of the country brought many problems for the land itself. The Interstate Commerce Act of 1887 was comprehensive in its language but had little power for many years. In 1890, the Sherman Anti-Trust Act prohibited industries to restrain trade, also an unenforceable law at the time and the third effort, came to life as an amendment. Only a few lines were devoted to giving the President the authority to hold safe certain land as part of the public domain. Little was accomplished by these laws at the time but they would surface later in the country's history.

Consumption rises each year, even in bad times. Food, water, energy, goods, manufactured hard materials increase, led by the growth in the world's population and the rise of third world countries to consumer status.

Ronald Wright speaks to climate change and the resultant weather instability causing a rise in droughts, floods, fires and hurricanes. Pollution and war add other factors. And even more, the overcrowding of some areas and the connection of all people by air travel invites a microbe to solve the problem of population density.

In the early 21st century, heat waves, droughts, floods and storms have made headlines. While the droughts in the American mid-west have not reached the proportions of the dust-bowl, we have had a wake-up call.

A look back to the thriving fishing trade of Maine and the maritimes is a lesson in point. The town that grew from the blessings conferred by the presence of the sardine is now a leader in fish farming. A good adaptation and a tribute to Down East ingenuity, but also a warning that the sea is less teaming with life than in the past. The staple fish for several continents, the cod, is now a delicacy and its price makes that clear. Fish and chips, or cod and fries, are now made with pollock.

The Government

The Supreme Court

Before leaving the White House in 1801, just as the century turned, John Marshall of Virginia was named Chief Justice of the United States by President John Adams. Marshall stayed in this office for almost 35 years. This gave full opportunity for him to give his own views on the Constitution legal status. In case after case, he proclaimed acts of state legislatures in violation of the Constitution and therefore, null and void. This constant testing of the strength of the Union and federal law is an issue over 200 years later. The Federal government through the Supreme Court, overcame the authority of states in issues of industry and labor in both interstate and foreign commerce.

The alterations in the Judicial Branch have been great in the years from John Marshall to John Roberts. Once a court with no home, it has become a powerful body with the ability to effect great changes in the country.

The Supreme Court in 2013 is a combination of older Justices and those who are very young. Those on the bench of SCOTUS who claim the title "originalists" include one Justice who argues that he can clearly discern the intent of the writers of the Constitution. Jeremy Waldron asks the question "Why are some among us so sure that reference back to the original intentions of the framers of our Constitution—men who lived in circumstances staggeringly different from our own—is a better source of wisdom than modern jurists who are fully acquainted with the distinctive conditions of polity and administration in 2012?" The question was posed in a review of two books published by Alan Ryan, in The New York Review of Books, February 21, 2013. Waldron's answer cites the need for an anchor in difficult times, one that gives precedents that insure our way of life is lasting. Waldron, a Professor at the NYU School of Law and Chichele Professor of, Social and Political Theory at All Souls College, Oxford, recommends Ryan's writings, most specifically, "On Politics".

In the 21st century, women sit on the Supreme Court. The women are liberal leaning and represent diversity on the Bench of our highest Judicial branch of government. Ruth Bader-Ginsberg, Elena Kagan and Sonia Sotomayor are women with voices to be heard.

In an article titled "Heavyweight" in the March 8, 2013 issue of the New Yorker, Jeffrey Toobin writes of Ruth Bader Ginsburg who took on the most important women's rights cases in the Courts history. In the 70's, she argued before the Court as a Columbia Law School professor. She co-founded the womens' rights project at the American Civil Liberties Union and fought for the Equal Protection Clause of the Fourteenth Amendment.

Her stance on Roe vs. Wade is an example of her conservative approach, allowing many voices to be heard in answer to difficult decisions such as abortion and now, same-sex marriage. The dissent she wrote in regards to the Lilly Ledbetter case was based in large part on federal procedures. Ginsburg spoke from the Bench to the passing of Title VII and the 1991 Civil Rights Act. She urged Congress to overturn the Court's decision and with the inauguration of Barack Obama, the Lilly Ledbetter Fair Pay Act of 2009 became the first piece of legislature he signed. 2013 marks her 20th year as a Supreme Court justice.

The Legislature

As of 2011, 18.3% of the 535 Congressional seats are held by women: 20 of the 100 Senate seats, and 78 of the 435 seats in the House of Representatives. Three women serve as delegates to the House, representing Guan, the Virgin Islands and Washington, D.C.

Many of the women hold leadership roles and chair committees. The Center for American Women and Politics keeps running records of women in government.

In addition to recording data on gender, the CAWP notes the seating of women of color, Hispanics and Asian Americans moving up in the ranks of governance.

Considering the more or less recent date of Women's Suffrage, the record is one to watch. It is quite possible that the Presidential election of 2016 will see a woman on the ballot.

The Executive Branch

Franklin Delano Roosevelt appointed Francis Perkins as head of the Department of Labor in 1933. The Cabinet position was a first, and only 13 years after women achieved the right to vote. The Center for American Women in Politics notes that to date in 2011, 43 women had held a total of 47 Cabinet level appointments.

It is interesting to see where the women are working when chosen for these slots. Of the 43, 14 were attorneys, 13 academics, 3 governors and 27 had held government offices.

The first Black President took office after a primary race with a woman. Barack Obama narrowly beat Hillary Clinton for the Democratic Party nomination. It was a difficult choice for many liberals. As Hillary put it later, there are now a thousand cracks in the glass ceiling holding a woman from the highest office.

Wars and Women

Wars were responsible for the rapid rise of women in a range of occupations. The Revolutionary War promoted the idea of women as those responsible for raising the citizens of the new country. As men left home to fight for long periods of time, past ideas that station in life was determined at birth and a firm belief in predestination were dropped in favor of the power of the mother to set children on the path of goodness and glory. Both the War of 1812 and most especially the Civil War clearly showed the capability of women to take on the chores once done by men. At this time, many of those duties were agricultural but they expanded during WW I and WWII into work places including factories, Universities and Corporations.

This does not suggest that women were immediately recognized as equals. Equal pay for equal work remains an issue in the 21st century. However, in 2013 women were no longer restricted to non-combat roles in the military, one of the last bastions of male dominance. As pointed out by many woman who made the military their career, a lack of combat experience severely restricted their rise to high rank. It also limited their influence on some of the on-going problems in the military forces.

Wars acted as catalysts for women from the 19th century until the 21st. As men left to fight as volunteers or as part of a draft, women took their places in farms, factories and businesses. They proved their ability but were paid less for the same work. The Lily Ledbetter law in the 21st century put businesses on notice—equal pay for equal work is now in effect.

In the time span that three women were born, lived and died, a war was just over or just beginning. The reasons differed in some respects but hubris infected each one. As in an election, everyone from Jefferson to Roosevelt felt that things would quickly end with the just combatant the victor.

Wars at home and those abroad affected the financial cycles of depression, recession, deflation and inflation. The policies of many administrations were brought to bear on these problems with both good and bad results. And it can be noted that history often repeats itself.

Gender Discrimination

Women's Rights were won after many struggles. The determination of rights in the home, the workplace and as individual is open. Margaret Sanger's clinics began to free women from the cycle of yearly pregnancies, Roe vs Wade showed the road smoothing, but in the elections of 2007 and 2012 the issue of the rights of the unborn trumped the rights of the pregnant woman for many candidates and their constituents. Others say woman will never have equal opportunity until they can control the number and the birth time of their children.

The rights of women are debated once again as some in the political arena are determined to venture into the private lives of women, denying abortions for any reason and blocking birth control. This social agenda became a large part of the Republican parties debate in the 2012 primaries and in the Presidential election, swinging most women's votes to the Democrats. The party of less government ventured into the private lives of families, not women alone, with predictable results. There are voices in the country today that plan to use government to regulate birth control, one large impediment to the rise of women to powerful positions. The number of abortions by dubious means in past years had given way to better medical solutions. The efforts to take funds away from Planned Parenthood affect women's health in many ways, birth control is a small part of their needs.

Conclusions

Issues For Future Generations

The February 2013 State of the Union Address by President Obama focussed on immigration, the budget, gun control, and same-sex marriage. Don't Ask Don't Tell is gone in the military but the States' legislatures differ on same-sex marriage. The Supreme Court will grapple with State laws in Hollingsworth v. Perry addressing California Proposition 8 that added an amendment to the state constitution defining marriage as a union between a man and a woman. The Court also will study the 1996 federal law that blocks Social Security benefit payments and other benefits to same sex couples married in states that permit gay unions.

Immigration continues as a major concern for Republicans hopeful of attracting Hispanic voters to the party and to others who want to stop the outflow of qualified experts who come to study, learn and then leave because there is no path to citizenship. Children who spend their lives here are another concern, they are Americans in every respect except birth place.

And there is other business on the burners in Washington, D.C. in 2013. Gun control is still under attack by right-wing politicians and those who feel it necessary to carry guns for self-protection from the madmen in the populace and from the government if it proves necessary. The difference in states and cities is remarkable. The rate of crime and gun related incidents in New York City goes steadily down under the push for gun control led by Mayor Bloomberg, and the state also is leading strong gun control laws. In Texas, there is no state required registration of guns, no waiting period for gun purchases and no limits on the type of number of guns owned. In an article in the February 18, 2013 USA Today by Rick Jervis, John Rosenthal, co-founder of the Newton, MA based Stop Gun Violence advocate group is quoted. Rosenthal states that the lack of gun laws in Texas make it an excellent source of guns for criminals everywhere. It does appear that some national law making is a necessity. It is in the offing but with dubious chances of success. At issue is the question of States' Rights. When do they conflict with the welfare of all?

The war in Afghanistan is winding down to a full withdrawal although there are many in the government and the public realm who anticipate fighting in Iran, Syria, North Korea and sites to be determined. Years without a war or military intervention are few and not surprisingly, the least occurred under a military man who warned the country about the military-industrial complex and involvement in overseas problems. You may first have thought of George Washington but the correct answer is Dwight Eisenhower. The United States spends more on its military budget than all the other countries in the world combined. At some point it is pertinent to ask why. In 2011, at a hearing of the House Armed Services Committee, protestors were carted away by the Capital Hill police. Nevertheless, the hearing spent hours discussing and defending the defense budget. A statement by Chair of the Joint Chiefs of Staff, General Martin Dempsey, deserves to be quoted: "I didn't become the chairman of the Joint Chiefs to oversee the decline of the Armed Forces of the United States, and an end state that would have this nation and its military not be a global power. That is not who we are as a nation." And so the isolationists of past, present and future are put on notice. Jill Lepore wrote of this in the January 28, 2013 New Yorker and asked the question, "Either the United States rules the world or Americans are no longer Americans?" Yet another question that needs an answer.

In the 21st century, the issue of secession is still an answer for some who have not quite understood the meaning of a freely elected President, a unified nation or treason. A week after the re-election of President Barack Obama, residents of 50 states had filed petitions to secede from the Union. The petitions were filed with digital signatures on the "We the People" online petition system and the Obama administration has promised a review. However, none of the Governors of the states involved have supported these efforts, even Rick Perry, Governor of Texas, who once suggested secession as a possibility.

Some specific historic events were highlighted in previous chapters because of their far reach from past to future.

Aaron Burr was tried for treason with the active support of a sitting President, Thomas Jefferson. The powers of the three branches of government shift with dominance by political parties and the swings in opinion of the people they represent. This trial brought the concept of secession to the fore early in the country's history and also prompted a Constitutional change in the voting procedure of President and Vice-President.

The War of 1812 linked the US with Europe once again. The position of England as the one strong deterrent to Napoleon's ambition would throw its shadow over events in the second World War when the United States backed Great Britain's struggle against Germany. This time, the alliance with England was not in doubt, and the need for a free Europe fully understood, if not until events touched the United States.

Captain Dreyfus died early in the 20th century, completely acquitted of the accusations leveled against him. But the holocaust followed in the 1930's with the deaths of many and the confiscation of so much. The creation of Israel gave hope of a homeland to the Jewish people, but the rights of that country are tested by their neighbors. Peace between Israel and Palestine is still in the future.

The Civil War left legacies far outreaching those of the Revolution. In 2013, Philadelphia, Mississippi elected a Black Mayor. This was the site of the murder of three young men who went to the south to address the continued racism so apparent to advocates of civil rights. There is progress, yes, but more young Black men are imprisoned or disenfranchised and unemployable because of minor infractions than whites. Efforts to affect election outcomes are based on gerrymandered districts in some states and a strong effort to end the Voting Rights Act is underway. As the country and the world applauded the second inauguration of Barack Obama, the ripples of the Civil War can sometimes be seen in a waving flag of Dixie or in a line of voters waiting over 7 hours to place their ballots. In the 1950's just three Republicans were part of the South's 109 congressmen—the solid south was Democrat. By 1964, Lyndon Johnson remarked that passing civil rights legislation would cost the Democratic Party the southern vote for a generation. George Packer notes in an article titled "Southern Discomfort" that Johnson was "too optimistic". For awhile, Packer notes that the south became the authentic America but it is now becoming isolated once again and in need of redefining Southern Morality.

There was a factory in Bangladesh in December, 2011, where about 5,000 workers, mostly women, were employed. The parent company holds GAP as one of its largest clients. Bangladeshi factories compete with India and China for their share of the garment trade. While buyers from Bangladesh increase, workers suffer. Improvements in working conditions are mostly the result of Western advocacy groups, over-sight by the International Labor Rights Forum and local protests. The progress is slow. Sub-contracting disconnects retailers from the manufacture of the garments.

In 1909, Louis Brandeis called "industrial democracy" the extension of bargaining to all workers, immigrants, citizens or not. The Wagner Act in 1935 codified many of his ideas although the Taft-Hartley Act modified some of the previous gains in worker rights. The power of unions is not as great as it was a few decade past and the plight of laborers in other countries is far from just.

Reading History Backwards: A Prologue

When needed, women can shoot predators, cook buffalo, wash diapers in cold water without soap, build homes, raise children while maintaining households, and build businesses. They can go to war and they can now change the course of elections.

The three Sarahs started this story but as the names change the themes remain the same. There has surely been progress for women and recognition of what they can achieve. In most cases, war was an impetus for the rise of women's rights but over time, the need for shelter expanded to mean more than a roof, food and clothing. Women needed shelter from the society for themselves and their children. They needed a voice to make their needs resound.

The Sarahs married coopers, farmers, fishermen, mariners, stevedores and risk-takers. The families all lived on the east coast and shared the life accented by water. They had different perspectives from the early settlers who moved west. The plethora of cultures, religions, and even languages always added to their ability to accept new ideas. And from memories and records two Sarahs exhibited a love of literature.

Ronald Wright speaks to Gauguin's questions to the nature of existence. His queries: Where do we come from? What are we? Where are we going? are seen in the mural he created after leaving the life of European civilization for Tahiti. Wright's theory is that if we can clearly understand what we are and what we have done, we can, most likely, guess where we are going. There is no doubt the past can be studied but what we are is still an open question. Will the mistakes and errors already completed be repeated, will we blunder once again on a new track, or will our world exist to improve the lives of all?

The pressing issues of the 21st century are well rooted in the 19th. Then, as now, the Constitution was a sacred document and the further the country moved from its first President and the founders, the more the "true" meaning of the Constitution was open to political interpretation. But many decades after the American Revolution the United States of America is one nation. Justice for all is still its goal.

Notes and References

The information on the family comes largely from the records researched by Joan Alexis Altgelt through Ancestry, its search engines, and the contacts it led to in present times. Joan managed to produce Bloodlines for all branches of the family and she located the maps that show the feasibility of early interactions. Joyce Emery Kinney of Eastport, Maine was a valuable resource in person and through her book, *Downeast People*. Town and State records from Maine were used to recreate past times for early ancestors but the family living in 2013 have filled in many of the blanks. Photographs were collected as family members searched for the past. The old shots, torn from really old albumns, were refurbished by Algis Balinskas, master of technology.

Eaarlier History books were used to connect more closely to the times.

I. The Nineteenth Century: A Global Picture

Africa And The Middle East: 1800-1914. Chapter 25. Pdf file

Columbia University. *Asia for Educators*. New York:2009

Ergang, Robert, PhD. *Europe In Our Time: 1914 To The Present*. New York: Scott, Foresman and Company, 1949, 87-97

Japan, 1800-1900 A.D. in *Heilbrunn Timeline of History,* New York. The Metropolitan Museum of Art:2000.

Japan:Memoirs of a Secret Empire. Timeline 1800's. PBS

Latin-American Economies and World Markets, 1820-1870.

McCourt, Mallachy. *History of Ireland*. Philadelphia, PA:2003, 298-299.

Marshall, Professor Peter. *British India And The 'Great Rebellion'. BBC:British History in Depth.*

Wallbank, Walter T. & Alastair M. Taylor. *Civilization: Past and Present*. Scott, Foresman and Company. New York: 1949, 365-366.

II. Pierre Du Sud and Port Royal

Belanger, Claude. "Political History of Canada" in *L'Encyclopédia de l'histoire du Québec*. Marianopolis College, 2005.

Genealogical Register of the Morang & Morong Family Originating in Maine: containing an account of Francis Morang (Francois Morin b. ca. 1742), his wife Rosalie Forest, the first of the family, their forebears and their descendants.

III. Lubec

Lender, Mark Edward and James Kirby. *Drinking in America: A History*. New York: The Free Press, 1982, 44-47

Multhop, Jennifer. "*Lubec: A Border Town Shaped by the Sea*." http://lubec. Mainememory.net/page/722.
   Multhop wrote the text for this article. Her sources are many and include local memories, published articles and newspaper accounts from the times.

Varney, George J. "History of Lubec, Maine". *A Gazetteer Of The State of Maine*. B.B. Russell, Publisher. Boston:1886.

IV. Sarah Morang and Nathaniel Mc Donald

Boyd, Amos. *Real People DownEast*. St. Croix Printing & Publishing co. Ltd., St. Stephen, N.B., 2002. 32-33. This book, written by Joyce Kinney of Eastport, Maine, is the product of many hours of researching through newspapers of the times and it is "dedicated to all newspaper editors, past and present, and to the editors, owners and staff of the DownEast Times." Joyce Kinney also researched and published the story of shipping from early times and her wealth of information on ships, their captains and crews, cargo, tonnage and destinations is carried over in this book. I wish it were longer.

Collins, Gail. *America's Women: Four Hundred Years of Dolls, Drudges, Helpmates, and Heroines*. New York: Harper Perennial, 2003, 125-126, 132-135

Maine Memory Network (http://www.mainememory. net/

Mintz, Steven. Housework in Late 19th Century America. Digital History: Back To The History of Private Life. Digital History Home:Using New Technologies to Enhance Teaching and Research. Up-dated November 19, 2012. With parts of Gail Collins' book, this makes a very complete record of the homemakers of the times.

Wilipedia:1795-1820 in Fashion

V. Education in the 19th century

Kilbey, William Henry, editor. *Eastport & Passamaquoddy: A Collection of Historical & Biographical Sketches.* Chapter VII. Daniel T. Granger. <u>Early Eastport Schools.</u> Eastport, Maine: Edward E. Shead & Co. 1888.

Jacoby, Susan. *The Great Agnostic: Robert Ingersoll and American Free Thought.* New Haven: Yale University Press, 2012, 106-107

Payne, Shannon. www7/mcguffey.html

Wesley, Edgar B. NEA: The First Hundred Years. New York:Harper & Brothers, 1957.

VI. The Nation

Crain, Caleb. "Unfortunate Events: What Was the War of 1812 Even About?" The New Yorker:October 22, 2012, 77-80.

Hopkins, J. Castell. "The War of 1812-15" in *The Story of the Dominion: Four Hundred Years in the Annals of Half a Continent.* Toronto, The John C. Winston Company, 1901, 183-207.

Newmyer, R. Kent. The Treason Trial of Aaron Burr: Law, Politics, and the Character Wars of the New Nation. Cambridge University Press. New York:2012, 22, 43, 47, 50-56, 71, 97, 174-179, 190, 200

The role of partisan politics strikes a rich note in 2012 although Dr. Newmyer allows the reader to find these similarities without editorial comment. Pages 147 and 205 define the partisan media and the winning of public opinion well. Most especially significant now are the passages on "haters" of the President both lawyers, reporter and public citizens. Luther Martin, a lawyer for Burr, was a passionate speaker. His speech is worth quoting: "He (President Jefferson) is no more than a servant of the people. He has assumed to himself the knowledge of the Supreme Being himself...." p.41, 98, 147–149, 190–200.

Taylor, Alan. *The Civil War of 1812: American Citizens, British Subjects, Irish Rebels, and Indian Allies.* New York: Knopf, 2010.
Taylor argues that 1812 was a Civil War in every sense with sentiments left over from the time of the American Revolution.

When The U.S. Invaded Canada. The Week. August 10, 2012.

Yale Biographical Dictionary of American Law; Burr, Aaron.

VII. Home in Eastport

Border Historical Society: Eastport.

Eastport History Collection. University of Maine. Memories, tapes, Interviews.

Genealogical Notes On the Eastport Maine Branch of The Emery Family. Compiles by R.C. Emery, 1950.

Maine Memory Network. (http://www.mainememory. net/

Mintz, Steven. Housework in Late 19th Century America. Digital History

Wikipedia: 1795-1820 In Fashion

VIII. The Civil War

Beard, Charles A. and Mary R. Beard. A Basic History of the United States. New York: The New Home Library. 1944, 246-271.

> Beard emphasizes Lincoln's appeals for compromise and his attempts to avoid war. He is also clear in showing Lincoln's desire to help reconstruction in the south—a bitter issue that almost saw the impeachment of President
>
> Johnson who took office after the assassination of Lincoln.

Boyd, Amos. 94-102.

Hymowitz, Carol and Michaele Weissman. A History Of Women In America. Bantam Books. New York:1978, 93, 94 148-149.

Maine In The Civil War. https://www.familysearch.org/learn/wiki/en/Maine Mintz.

Trethewey, Natasha. *Native Guard.* Houghton Mifflin Company. Boston.New York: 2006, 48.

Weaver, C.P., ed. *Thank God My Regiment and African One: The Civil War Diary of Colonel Nathan W. Daniels.* Baton Rouge: Louisiana State University Press, 1998.

Wesley, Edgar B. *NEA: The First Hundred Years:The Building Of The Teaching Profession.* New York: Harper & Brothers Publishers, 1957, 10–12

IX. Maine to New York

Brookhaven Census.
"Brookhaven, N.Y." Wikipedia.org/wiki/Brookhaven_New York. Last modified on 8 July, 2012.

Other sources: http://www.brookhaven.org.

Department of the Interior, Bureau of Pensions. 1915
Ergang, Robert. Europe In Our Time: 1914 To The Present. New York: D.C. Hath and Company: 1953, 87-97.

Federal Census. 1910

Fox, Stephen. *Transatlantic.* N.Y.: Harper Collins, 2003. Pp 401.

The story of the Cunard family links the fortunes of the Loyalists to the Canadian maritimes and England. The base for this shipping Empire was Liverpool but its impact on the U.S. was immense.

"On the Irish Waterfront." Wikipedia with sources listed: Montgomery, David, Iven Bernstein, and Robert Greenhalgh Albion (with collaboration of Jennie Barnes Pope.)

New York Times. "Doors Were Locked, Say Rescued Girls". March 27, 1911 (no attribution)

Robbins, Tom. "A Century After Triangle, Unions Battle New Fires." *Forward.com*. March 25, 2011.

Woodrow Wilson. "A History of the American People," 517–532.

History of Long Island. Wikipedia.org/wiki/History of Long Island.

X. Sarah Emery Hughes

Ancestry.com

Family records/letters/memories

Census Records

XI. Moving On

Mc Auliffe, Mary. Dawn of the Belle Epoque. Rowman & Littlefield Publishers, Inc. lanham, Maryland: 2011, 291-299.
> Mary McAuliffe, author of La Belle Epoch, uses her PhD in history to build a story of amazing talents and artistic expression in a city with foreshadowing's of the 1930's as well a a lasting legacy of paintings, sculpture, music and theater.

Wilkes, Donald E. *Dreyfus Case Began a Century Ago*. Georgia Advocate. University of Georgia School of Law. Georgia:1994, 29

Wallbank, Walter T. and Alastair M. Taylor. Civilization: Past and Present. Scott, Foresman and Company. New York:1949, 365-366.

Family records and memories

XII. Sarah's Daughters

Family records

XIII. The Economy As History

Conte. Christopher. <u>An Outline of the U.S. Economy.</u> Washington, D.C.: U.S. Dept. Of State, International Information Programs, 2001.

The Federal Reserve Board. *The Structure of the Federal Reserve System.* Updated July 8, 2003. Federal Reserve:online government.

Ferguson, Thomas. (see Wikipedia.org/index Thomas Ferguson.

Foroohar, Rana. *The Risks of Reviving A Revived Economy.* TIME. NY, NY. November 19, 2012, 35.

Gordon, John Steele. *The Business of America.* New York: Walker & Company, 2001.

Kothari, Preeti Loonker, Ahluwalia, Poonam, Nema, Arvind K._*A grey system approach for forecasting disposable computer waste quantities: a case study of Delhi* International Journal of Business Continuity and Risk Management. Volume 2, Number 3, September 2011, 203-218.

National Bureau of Economic Research. *U.S. Business Cycle Expansions and Contractions.* Cambridge, Mass. Press release, September 20, 2010.

Outline of the U.S. Economy. America.gov. September, 2009.

Random History.com. *Of Revolution, Glory, and Uncertainty: A History of the U.S. Economy.*

Samuelson, Paul A. Economics: An Introductory Analysis. McGraw-Hill Book Company, Inc. New York:1951, 316

The Federal Reserve Board. *"The Structure of the Federal Reserve System."* Updated July 8, 2003. Federal Reserve:online government publications.

Wallbank, T. Walter and Alastair M. Taylor. *Civilization: Past and Present.* Scott, Foresman and Company. New York: 1949, 365–366

Watkins, Thayer. San Jose State University Department of Economics. Applet-magic.com. Silicon Valley & Tornado Alley USA.

Wilkes, Donald E. *Dreyfus Case Began a Century Ago.* Georgia Advocate. University of Georgia School of Law. Georgia:1994, 29.
  The article by Donald E. Wilkes, Professor of Law, was written to mark the date when a century past, Alfred Dreyfus was convicted of treason. Although not fully stated, it is clear that Dreyfus was Jewish incited public opinion and assured the ease of his conviction of flimsy charges.

"Doors Were Locked, Say Rescued Girls," New York Times, March 27, 1911. (no attribution).

Robbins, Tom. "A Century After Triangle, Unions Battle New Fires." *Forward.com.* March, 25, 2011.

XIV. Legacies and Progress

Collins, Gail. *As Texas Goes*. New York/London: Liveright Publishing Corporation, 2012, 3,4

Packer, George. *Southern Discomfort*. The New Yorker. January 21, 2013.

References

Beard, Charles A. and Mary R. Beard. A Basic History Of The United States.

The New Home Library. New York:1944.

Collins, Gail. *America's Women*. Harper Perennial, New York. 2004.

Genealogical Notes On The Eastport, Main Branch Of The Emery Family. Compiled by R.C. Emery, 1950

Genealogical Register of the Morang & Morong family originating in Maine: containing an account of Francis Morang (Francois Morin b. ca. 1742), his wife Rosalie Forest, the first of the family, their forebears and their descendents.

Lender, Mark Edward and James Kirby. Drinking in America: A History. The Free Press. New York:1982 pp 44-47

Lepore, Jill. "Vast Designs" New Yorker. October 29, 2007

Maine Memory Network (http://www.mainememory. net/)

Payne, Shannon. www7/mcguffey.html

Wikipedia: 1795-1820 in Fashion

References

Ergang, Robert, Ph.D. Europe In Our Time: 1914 To The Present. D.C. Heath and Company, New York:1953. Pp 87-97.

Wallbank, Walter T, and Alastair M. Taylor. Civilization Past and Present. Scott, Foresman and Company. New York:1949 pp365-366

Bibliography

"Africa And The Middle East: 1800-1914." Chapter 25, Pdf file.

Asia for Educators. New York:Columbia University Press, 2009.

Beard, Charles A. and Mary R. Beard. *A Basic History of the United States.* New York: The New Home Library, 1944.

Belanger, Claude. "Political History of Canada". *In L'Encyclopedia de l'histoire du Quebec.* Marianopolis College, 2005.

Collins, Gail. *America's Women.* New York: Harper Perennial, 2004.

Collins, Gail. *As Texas Goes*. New York/London: Liveright Publishing Corporation. 2012.

Conte, Christopher. "An Outline of the U.S. Economy." Washington, D.C.: U.S. Department of State, International Information Programs.

Crain, Caleb. "Unfortunate Events:What Was The War of 1812 Even About?" New York: The New Yorker: October 22, 2012.

Donovan, James. *The Blood of Heroes*. N.Y.,New York: Little, Brown & Co., 2012.

Ergang, Robert, Ph.D. *Europe In Our Time: 1914 To The Present*. New York:D.C. Heath and Company, 1953.

Fox, Stephen. *Transatlantic*. N.Y.: Harper Collins, 2003.

Federal Reserve Board. "The Structure of the Federal Reserve System." Up-dated July 8, 2003 Federal Reserve:online government publications.

Genealogical Notes on The Eastport Maine Branch of the Emery Family. Compiled by R.C. Emery, 1950.
Genealogical Register of the Morang & Morong Family Originating in Maine: Containing an account of Francis Morang (Francois Morin b. ca. 1742), his wife Rosalie Forest, the first of the family their forebears and their descendants.

Gordon, John Steele. *The Business of America*. New York: Walker & Company, 2001.

Hopkins, J. Castell. "The War Of 1812-15." in *The Story Of The Dominion: Four Hundred Years In The Annals of Half a Continent*. Toronto: The John C. Winston Company, 1901.

Hymowitz, Carol and Micaele Weissman. *A History of Women In America*. New York: Bantam Books, 1978.

Jacoby. Susan. *The Great Agnostic: Robert Ingersoll and American Freethought*. New Haven/ London:Yale University Press, 2012.

Lender, Mark Edward and James Kirby. *Drinking in America: A History*. New York:The Free Press, 1982.

Lepore, Jill. "Vast Designs". New York; The New Yorker, October 29, 2007.

Maine Memory Network (http://www.mainememory. net/

Marshall, Professor Peter. *British India And The 'Great Rebellion'*. BBC: British History In Depth.

Mintz, Steven. "Housework in Late 19th Century America." *Digital History: Back to the History of Private Life. Digital History Home*: Using New Technologies to

Enhance Teaching and Research. Up-dated November 19, 2012.

Outline of the U.S. Economy. America.gov. September, 2009.

Payne, Shannon. www7/mcguffey.html

Random History.com 2007-20013. *Of Revolution, Glory, and Uncertainty A History of the U.S. Economy.*

Samuelson, Paul A. *Economics: An Introductory Analysis.* New York: McGraw Hill Book Company, Inc.:1951.

Taylor, Alan. *The Civil War of 1812: British Subjects, Irish Rebels, & Indian Allies.* New York:Knopf, 2010.

Trethewey, Natasha. *Native Guard.* Boston.New York: Houghton Mifflin Company. 2006.

Varney, George J. "History of Lubec, Maine" *A Gazetteer Of The State Of Maine.* Boston: B.B. Russell, Publisher, 1886.

Wallbank, Walter T, and Alastair M. Taylor. Civilization Past and Present. New York:Scott, Foresman and Company, 1949.

Watkins, Thayer. San Jose State University Department of Economics. Applet-magic.com. Silicon Valley & Tornado Alley USA.

Weaver, C.P., ed. *Thank God My Regiment an African One: The Civil War Diary of Colonel Nathan W. Daniels.* Baton Rouge: Louisiana State University Press, 1998.

Wesley, Edgar B. *NEA:The First Hundred Years:The Building Of The Teaching Profession.* New York:Harper & Brothers Publishers, 1957.

Wikipedia: 1795–1820 in Fashion.